LET'S TALK!

LET'S TALK!

A GUIDE TO AWKWARD CONVERSATIONS AND UNIFYING DIALOGUE IN THE CHURCH

TODD PHEIFER

Let's Talk

Published in the United States of America by Credo House Publishers, a division of Credo Communications LLC, Grand Rapids, Michigan
credohousepublishers.com

ISBN: 978-1-62586-244-0

Cover and interior design and layout by Frank Gutbrod
Editing by Donna Huisjen

Printed in the United States of America
First edition

CONTENTS

Preface 1

Chapter 1: *The family of God* 5

Chapter 2: *A very brief history of conflict* 19

Chapter 3: *Desires for redemption* 33

Chapter 4: *The belief in dialogue* 47

Chapter 5: *Confronting biases and limitations* 63

Chapter 6: *Curiosity and paradigm shifts* 77

Chapter 7: *Emotions, distractions, and listening* 93

Chapter 8: *Communities and echo chambers* 109

Chapter 9: *Defining our terms* 125

Chapter 10: *What is the plan?* 141

Chapter 11: *Some thoughts on technology* 157

Chapter 12: *Impasses, detours, and letting go* 173

Chapter 13: *A work in progress* 187

Bibliography 203

PREFACE

Each day we wake up and are faced with a shifting laundry list of global challenges. Today, these issues include climate change, widespread generational poverty, the struggle between democracy and authoritarianism, mass incarceration, identity politics, and how all those factors contribute to our personal existence. For most of us, each day represents a new opportunity to interact with an unpredictable world and a chance to continue living dangerously. The fundamental decision for each of us is whether to engage with new ideas or retreat into the safety of roads we have already walked.

Followers of Christ are not exempt from these daily dilemmas, which is why this book is written as a challenge to Christians and the universal church. The challenge is to live in a true community, namely the body of believers. To do this, we need to be better at dialogue. Period. This book reflects a belief that productive conversation and a better reality of mutual understanding can occur. This is not to suggest that there will be a point in the future when the church collectively sits in a circle, holding hands and singing with one voice on this side of life. This is still a sinful world, and there is always work to be done that will be complicated by our fallen natures. Conflict will remain, and, just as with new issues, there will be fresh disagreements.

Perhaps you and your community have already developed an atmosphere of robust dialogue, but I would like to start this book by cautioning you against a belief that you have somehow *arrived.* In addition, too often people read books like this, agree with the general content, and then assume that it should be applied to someone else. In other words, we think about the person who would really benefit from reading this type of book, which we hope will be coupled with a strong sense of self-conviction (mostly on their part). Whether we apply that same thinking to ourselves is another matter entirely. What I hope you take from this book is that, no matter how many conversations we facilitate, we can always meet new people, explore additional ideas, and listen to the stories of real individuals.

At the risk of overemphasizing my own self-importance (or yours), existing in this world and pursuing measurable change begins with me. This isn't to say that the world revolves around my life. Nor does it imply that I am singularly responsible for fixing everything. The key idea is that I always need to learn more, make additional life adjustments, and be ready to change myself. Asking the world around me to make all the changes while I stay the same simply won't do. You may nod in agreement at this obvious statement, but the reality is that humans are often far more selfish than we let on. We don't like change, we avoid hard work, and, if we are transparent, we must admit that we want the world to revolve around our needs. In some cases, we will do whatever it takes to fashion around us a world that focuses on us and the desires of our hearts. Dispute that mindset if you wish, but human history has produced many individuals who have made decisions that have benefited their singular existence. We aren't just talking about the so-called notorious villains, dictators, and heinous criminals of different ages. Sin touches every one of us. There have, of course, also been love, compassion, selflessness, and altruism displayed by many people, and we will get to that. For now, what we must face is the cold darkness of our own sinful nature to appreciate the hope of the gospel message, as well as the redemptive possibilities that can occur in a fallen world that still has great potential to glorify God. This may be a rough way to get started, but dialogue and understanding begin with our own willingness to grow.

Each chapter starts with what I have labeled an Honesty Check. That concept should be somewhat self-explanatory, but let's just say that honesty is never guaranteed with humans. These are simple questions that I would like you, the reader (or a small group), to ponder for as long as needed. I don't want you to be burdened by constant doubt or a nagging sense that you can't do anything right, but self-reflection can be an important exercise to pursue as we seek out unity with our fellow humans. For this step to be most effective, you may find it necessary to ask family, friends, "frenemies," or co-workers to provide you with candid feedback. Ideally, you might ask people who will be honest! Take their responses with grace, dignity, and an acceptance that we all have more to learn. If anything, a request for feedback may lead to a thoughtful and productive conversation and a desire to work together toward kingdom goals in the future. That, my esteemed reader, is the point.

Before we jump in, it is also important to recognize that we all see the world differently. Put another way, not everyone processes their reality the same, nor do all people gravitate toward deep thoughts about life, the universe, and everything in it. This doesn't have to do with intelligence, though we should recognize that humanity represents a spectrum of cognitive skills. What we are talking about is the human desire for simplicity. We may say that we like a variety of choices and new ideas, but our behaviors suggest that we often feel most comfortable when we can establish a consistent worldview and build a predictable lifestyle around our core ideology. The goal of this book is not to suggest that your worldview is wrong or that you should reevaluate every one of your tenets. Rather, I am suggesting that rock-solid truth should be something we can not only defend but also succinctly articulate because we know *why* our beliefs exist.

With that said, let us get started. Happy conversing. Happy listening. Happy understanding.

1

THE FAMILY OF GOD

HONESTY CHECK

Is your biological family a source of joy, sorrow, or some combination of the two? Does your family (in part or as a whole) get along? What does getting along mean to you? Is your family able to talk about deeper issues, or do you get along by avoiding certain awkward topics? What topics are difficult for your family to discuss? Has your family atmosphere been consistent over time, or were there particular events that changed the dynamics?

This book is about meaningful dialogue in the church and how conversations can lead to greater depth of relationship and discipleship and a more unified vision of sharing the gospel. The word *dialogue* can mean many things. Some conversations between people who are part of the church community are deep, vulnerable, and insightful. Others are surface level, consisting of verbal exchanges that occur after a worship service about sports, weekly schedules, . . . and perhaps, just maybe, the sermon. The point is that we, the universal church, can do better. We must do better. We are biblically called to do better. So, let's talk about how we are going to improve the quality and impact of our dialogue. Not to undersell this content, but a book can't force you to talk with others. That said, I feel that I can give you some insights and tips on how to get the conversation going, which I pray will lead to greater depth of relationship and excitement for ministry. Let us start with a discussion of family, but perhaps not the family that immediately comes to mind.

THE FAMILY OF GOD

Families fight from time to time. This is true for even the most loving, supportive families. With all the different elements of a complex society, some level of interpersonal conflict is quite possibly unavoidable even for the deepest of human relationships. In many ways, some may suggest that genuine depth in relationships is not achieved until people work through a given number of differences and conflicts. For obvious reasons conflict can be frightening, which is why humans actively avoid fights or in some cases even differences of opinion. To be fair, this is a difficult way to start a book, and I am certainly not suggesting that you go out and start a fight so that you can achieve a higher level of relational intimacy. The reader might protest, "Hey, why start so negatively? Can't we talk about positive family aspects like love? Affection? Loyalty? The happy bonds that exist primarily among blood relatives?

Okay, fine. As much as I want to set a tone of realism, there are many positive aspects of family we should celebrate. I will start the chapter over again, or at least pretend to begin again. Families are *wonderful*. Love. Joy. Harmony. Positive pride. Shared memories. Legacy. The best things about the human experience. Power of genealogy. Is that better? Despite the challenges of family, it is fair to suggest that these beloved people often represent our core inner circle. When you think about who you might defend more than anyone else in the world (or who might most readily come to your aid in a crisis), immediate family members often come to mind. These individuals have special titles, endearing nicknames, unique statuses, shared secrets, and particular privileges in society. Families are often the focal point when celebrating major and minor holidays; birthdays; career milestones; weddings; and, ultimately, funerals. People around the world die every moment of every day, but we hardly take notice. However, when someone close to you passes away, your individual life may never again be the same.

Granted, these elements are also why family disagreements are some of the most painful aspects of the human experience. The people who supposedly love you the most can also hurt you the most deeply. Family members who are estranged from each other can experience deep, painful rifts that might linger for years, if not a lifetime. There are, unfortunately, some situations in which there is no greater pain than the hurt caused by a family member. The family, therefore, is a bit of a dichotomy that exists on a very broad spectrum of love and hatred. There are deep, unbreakable bonds but also the potential for seemingly irreparable rifts.

So, let's put this complex social construct together, if possible. The thing with dichotomies is that they can represent an ongoing tension or, in some cases, an almost whiplash reality of opposing experiences. As mentioned, families can represent the most crucial connections in life and be a focal point of happiness and positive pride. At the same time, families can be sources of tremendous pain and the cause of daily suffering that lasts far too long. The key element is that even in warm, loving families, there is conflict that is the result of humans attempting to live together in some level of harmony. Families fight, and love, all under the same roof. Let's talk about that. Really, it is okay.

GOD'S BIG, BEAUTIFUL, DYSFUNCTIONAL COLLECTION OF CHILDREN

The "family of God" is admittedly a more spiritual label than a biological one. If we go back far enough in time, we can connect branches in the extensive forests of family trees throughout human history. However, this practice can become cumbersome very quickly once we start getting into once, twice, and three-times-removed cousins, blended families, and lost records. When we think of God as our spiritual Father, the concept of brothers and sisters in Christ can be a beautiful categorization of deep relationships that transcend all demographics. Also, no genealogical research is required to establish official connections. Why? The simple reason is that this family is born of something different.

Imagine human beings from every walk of life, culture, age, education, and economic condition being invited to participate not simply in a communal religious experience but as a family. Imagine God with open arms, ushering them into His house. God exchanges soiled rags for new, clean robes; gives names; and bestows privileges. These actions are done in the name of love and in union with His eldest Son. That is the big, but, most importantly, the beautiful part of being in the family of God. We may see only glimpses of this ultimate existence during our earthly life, but the point is that we must make the most of time and live together in focused unity.

The presence and amazement of this family should instill in us a sense of perpetual thanksgiving and a daily quest to invite others. As C. S. Lewis wrote in *Mere Christianity*, "If Christianity is true, then why are not all Christians nicer than all non-Christians?" If Christians believe that they are saved by grace, shouldn't we live lives of daily gratitude, love, and service to our fellow human beings? Shouldn't we live out the fruit of the Spirit (Galatians 5:22–23) and treat each other accordingly? Why are we not taking every opportunity to unite as the family of God so that we can go out and say to others, "Come, there is room at the table"? If only it were that simple. Maybe it is.

Are there Christ followers and communities of believers that love and support each other, hold each other accountable with grace, and joyfully savor praise and fellowship while continually sharing the gospel with others and addressing the tangible hurts of society? Yes! When this existence develops in a church community, it is a beautiful thing and a sight to behold. Unfortunately, we Christians are not always the best of people. Author Dan Kimball wrote a book titled *They Like Jesus but Not the Church: Insights from Emerging Generations*. I encourage you to read the whole book, but the title may give away the focus of the content. We, the church, don't consistently display love and harmony with one another, and the world sees how we act in our various environments.

In more pragmatic terms, the world sees the church bickering, like children in a public setting. We as the church need to own our behavior and how we collectively act toward one another. It may be our practice to refer to the church as God's family or as the house of God. However, much as with many dysfunctional earthly houses and families, we aren't always the most unified, hospitable, or inviting of destinations. It doesn't have to be that way. Chances are you have experienced homes in which you felt a sense of belonging, and others where you have not. If a nonaffiliated person were to walk into your church, what kind of family would they find?

MARCIA, MARCIA, MARCIA!

Children who grew up in Western culture in the 1970s may have been exposed to the popular situation comedy *The Brady Bunch*. The plot was reasonably simple. A single dad with three boys marries a single mom with three girls. Add in a sassy cook/housekeeper and a dog, and you've got yourself a recipe for seemingly clean family conflict (complete with laugh track). The show was entertaining because people could relate to the more innocent aspects of daily drama within a busy household.

Because the show was a thirty-minute comedy (including commercials), there was little time to develop a complex plot. As a result, there was a consistently simple resolution. The show had few cliffhangers and virtually no unresolved or lingering conflicts. We knew that there was standard animosity between the siblings, but it was playful, and this was a limited television universe. If we are honest, the fights were the best. When Peter bounces the football off Marcia's nose in the episode "The Subject Was Noses," that was television gold even though in real life it might have created an atmosphere of genuine frustration and anger that wouldn't have been resolved by the commercial break.

As mentioned earlier, some of the hardest, longest conflicts are between family members, both biological and spiritual. If you don't speak to a high school classmate after you graduate, it might not be a big deal. The argument with the random stranger on the street can be easily forgotten within minutes. However, not speaking to a family member for an extended period can create an immense amount of pain. As far as we know, the Brady family always worked things out and had a good laugh about their minor family drama. Real-life conflict does not resolve so easily. If one of the Brady kids were to have been estranged from the rest of the cast for multiple seasons, this would probably have clashed with the light, comedic tone of the show. After all, it was a *show*.

Do we feel the same pain about our brothers and sisters in Christ with whom we do not find harmony? When there is conflict in the family of God, does it cause us the same grief as when we have experienced fights in our own home? When Christians gather, do we have a Brady-like approach to conflict whereby we seek to simply get through thirty minutes together before moving on to a different show? Or do we view our fellow church attender with the same indifference as we might a stranger on the street? This is a serious question, and one we all must answer as we interact with our brothers and sisters. If we are honest (there is that word again), would we prefer our church gatherings to resemble a warm-hearted, playful sitcom where conflict is either minimal or easily resolved? Or are we willing to deal with tougher issues, explore characters in more depth, and ultimately accept some unresolved episodes?

If your church family/congregation were a television show, in what genre would it be? Also, what would be included in the plot synopsis? Would a viewer find your family/congregation to be compelling, or would they quickly change the channel?

WELCOME TO WORSHIP—PLEASE SMILE

The worship service is often a focal point in evangelical circles, as people from all walks of life gather for singing, prayer, a sermon, and perhaps some fellowship before or afterward. There are other elements of the liturgy that vary, depending on the denomination, and can include times of confession or lament, communion, baptisms, and offerings of various types. Some gatherings are more interactive than others, but it isn't difficult for an individual to attend a worship service and remain a quiet, passive observer.

In some ways, one could draw a parallel between the weekly worship service and an episode of *The Brady Bunch*. At a worship gathering, there are often smiles; handshakes; and, in some congregations, an almost encouraged projection of happiness. Positivity is not necessarily mandated, but in some places there is a definite sense that it is preferred. Some pastors mix a few jokes into the sermon to keep the studio audience engaged and the content palatable. Real issues are not necessarily discussed among the congregants. There may be serious themes of faith in the sermon or prayers, and some discussion may happen in Bible study, but there are also church attenders who definitively shy away from content that is too close to the evening news or deeper personal reflection. Some gatherers will suggest that the pastor preach straight from the Scripture and not mix in too much social or political application.

In these gatherings we may receive the Word of God and sing powerful songs that speak of life-altering commitment to our all-in faith, but after that is done we may grab some coffee and cookies before heading out to resume our normal routine. We enjoy our spiritual episode for the week, but then it is time to move on. The family of God gathers for a posed spiritual family photo opportunity of sorts and then puts on our so-called real clothes before returning to what we really want to do. A sense of tranquility is maintained, but depth can, at times, be lacking.

Admittedly, this is a somewhat negative description of a stereotyped church body. By God's grace, there are many worship and church family gatherings that are beautiful representations of God's children gathering at the foot of His throne to give Him all the praise and glory He deserves. Some services are times of genuine worship, lament, and sincere reflection before attendees reenter their daily service to the kingdom. Members of some communities recognize that the worship gathering is not primarily a time for them to be fed. Rather, it is a time to truly worship and be reminded of the awesome and amazing responsibilities of fulfilling the Great Commission.

There are family photos that are a real representation beyond posed, forced smiles. Do the family of God in your typical worship setting and the average attender of your service experience that kind of transparency? Does your congregation create an atmosphere in which people can freely share not just joy but also sorrow and questions about complex issues? If the church holds a community event, does everyone sit with their friends, or is there an atmosphere of welcoming hospitality, paired with a desire to enfold new people?

KINSHIP AND OTHER CONNECTIONS

What we must ask ourselves as Christ followers (and ultimately as the church universal) is this: Do we truly buy into the idea of a spiritual family, and are we willing to see the entire convoluted group as even more important than our close biological connections? Will we put up with the drama that can sometimes occur and the dysfunctional relationship that still represents beauty because we are joined together by common faith? This is a crucial question that must be answered, and one that can have a profound impact on the success of eventual dialogue. One of the challenges of human existence is that we sometimes differentiate between what we say we believe in and how we live our actual lives. Unfortunately, there are many individuals who are unable to recognize this dichotomy. Whether it is from shame, embarrassment, or just a strong sense of self-assurance, we struggle with admitting our faults to ourselves and others. Therefore, if you ask people whether they see believers around the world as family members, they might nod assuredly, the same way people often do in a Bible study or sermon. There is often an expectation as Christians that we will agree with seemingly obvious tenets of the faith. However, is this lived out? That might be something entirely different.

The church as our spiritual family manifests in a variety of ways, and this idea forces us to constantly examine different social norms. For example, there is much historical division in society regarding the cultural structures of race and ethnicity. In his book *One Blood*, John Perkins talks about race as being a social construct, pointing out that we need to constantly strive for a sense of unity rather than focusing on our differences. We wish it were that simple, but that is where hope must be our constant companion. Likewise, in his book *Tattoos on the Heart*, Father Greg Boyle talks about the idea of kinship when approaching others. Instead of seeing someone through the lens of a particular status—such as that of a gang member or a homeless person—see them as a brother or sister in Christ. That individual is family. Your family. My family.

Granted, this kinship and family of God idea can be hard to force. We just don't feel a connection with that many people. I could say to you, "Hey, look! See that random stranger on the street? That is your brother or sister in Christ!" If I did, you might acknowledge the cognitive idea and even agree in your mind. However, would you feel the same sense of love, devotion, and commitment to that person that you do to your immediate, biological family? Doubtful. I'm not saying that I would, either. This is an ongoing challenge, but one we must commit to every day as we engage with people and new ideas.

We also must remember that some people don't feel much of a connection with anyone else, for a variety of reasons. This may be because love in their life has been lacking or pain has been all too abundant. People may talk about the difference between their head and heart when it comes to how things resonate with them. Even though there isn't a biological defense for this type of phraseology, we understand that simply grasping a concept does not mean that it will infuse our sense of self or core perspective on the world. Of course, we should love our neighbor as ourselves. The problem is that our neighbor is annoying. How do we deal with that?

A FEW GOALS

I have a few goals for this book. One is to simply promote and encourage dialogue, first within the church but, ultimately, to be more in harmony as we share the good news of the gospel. Obviously, we hope to do those things in tandem, and both can be elusive constructs. Maybe you get along fine with people in your faith community, and that is great. What I would ask you is this: How deep are those relationships? Have you had some complicated discussions about biblical interpretation and application of Scripture to the nuanced issues of your current society? How often do you engage in thoughtful dialogue with your brothers and sisters over topics that may at times be a bit uncomfortable? If you are honest, do you tend to seek out like-minded people?

A secondary goal is to convince you that better harmony is possible if you are committed to pursuing deeper, more transparent relationships over time. Because of sin, there will always be barriers, and we must recognize that building loving relationships is a daily exercise of dying to self. This is not an easy process. Oftentimes, we just don't have the energy or capacity to delve deeper. Therefore, many people (myself included) can be prone to keeping a few friends close and a lot of so-called friends (truthfully, acquaintances) on a more surface level. It is just easier to be civil and then go home, but this does not necessarily build strong bridges of friendship, support, and faith accountability.

I will suggest in this book some practical tools for dialogue, along with some observed barriers that can be addressed. However, application of these ideas will work only if you are willing to engage in a level of self-reflection and critique. As I mentioned in the preface, at the beginning of each chapter there will be a question (or up to a few of them) under the heading of Honesty Check. Again, I encourage you to read these questions carefully, engage in some honest assessment, and seek the counsel of others who will give you candid feedback as to how you process those questions. The same goes for the discussion questions at the end of each chapter, which may be used for personal reflection or a group discussion. I am not trying to convince you that you are a horrible person or that you should walk through life with a sense of self-loathing. The point is that we all have a role in the current state of conflict within the church. No one likes to raise their hand and say "My bad." However, on some level we all need to do it.

As we talk about, well, talking, keep thinking about this concept of the family of God. Are we unified, or aren't we? Is this just one of those nice, churchy things to say that don't get applied once we exit the doors of the sanctuary? In the process of writing this book, I bounced ideas off a variety of people. One individual asked why I was focusing on just the church and not the broader world. After all, the sum of humanity could certainly improve on their dialogue, regardless of ideology. That is a good question, but the answer is reasonably simple. As the church, we need to do better. We are in possession of the greatest news ever heard, and it is our job as the body of Christ to share it. To do that, shouldn't we do our best to get on the same page with as many topics as possible? Or at least in the same library?

I don't expect this book to be a conduit for a quickly united church, singing together in beautiful harmony and efficiently turning a fallen world into a loving utopia. Interpersonal conflict will remain until Christ returns. Period. That said, we can seek to redeem (chapter 3) during our short time on this planet. A pastor friend of mine once said, "Conflict is painful, sometimes unresolvable, but never without hope." I pray that you approach the possibility of better dialogue in the church with a sense of hope. That same pastor also said, "The hope of spiritual friendship is not that it lasts forever, but that it bears much fruit." Let us go on a journey together and explore ways in which we, the body of Christ, may more fully share what is in our hearts so that we can channel that energy into sharing the gospel. Ready or not, here we go.

PRACTICAL TIP

Make a list of conflicts (large and small) you may have had with family, close friends, or fellow church members. Write down the issue, the timetable of the conflict, how it started, how it was resolved (if it was), and how each perspective was presented and defended. Reflect on your feelings toward each conflict that you write down.

DISCUSSION QUESTIONS

1. Why can conflicts between family members be so intense and last for so long?
2. Why do people assemble family tree records, and what do those projects signify?
3. Do you think of the universal church as your family? Or do you consider even your local congregation this way?
4. What would it take for you to feel a sense of kinship with certain people, particularly with individuals you are not particularly close to now? Are these obstacles different for fellow church members?

2

A VERY BRIEF HISTORY OF CONFLICT

HONESTY CHECK

When you think about conflict between humans as a general idea, can you identify some core issues or factors that cause strife between individuals and groups? How do you personally deal with conflict? In general, do you feel that people are better or worse at conflict resolution today? Explain.

The Bible is the inspired Word of God, but this doesn't change the fact that this book is filled with stories of conflict. God is not the problem. We are. In Genesis 3:1 we are introduced to the serpent, and almost immediately the rhetoric begins. The verse says, "Now the serpent was more crafty than any other beast of the field that the LORD God had made. He said to the woman, 'Did God actually say, "You shall not eat of any tree in the garden"'?"

If we did not know the context of this verse, we might think that the serpent is innocently looking for clarification. There are plenty of instances in which people want to make sure that information as they have heard or understood it is correct, which prompts certain types of clarifying questions. To a certain extent, our education system teaches thoughtful skepticism, and children from an early age are encouraged to check sources and verify accuracy. We often refer to this as critical thinking, and it is something we wish for all people to develop to a certain extent.

The problem preventing our taking the serpent's words at face value is that we understand the larger context of this Bible passage. This verse provides us with a question that could, upon further scrutiny, be described as loaded or rhetorical. Unfortunately, the serpent is Satan, the master of lies. The serpent is not simply expressing curiosity, nor is the serpent allowing for the possibility that there is new knowledge for him to obtain. While he might have innocently suggested otherwise if the question had been answered differently by Eve, it is not hard to conclude that a definitive agenda is in the works. Whenever someone says "I was just asking," we may feel as though there is a different question being shrouded by a more palatable inquiry. With this Scripture the fall of humanity is in motion, and division between God and people caused by sin has been introduced. Sadly, it did not take long for humans to take a wrecking ball to God's beautiful creation. We can blame the serpent if we wish, but, ultimately, the decision to defy God starts and ends with people.

BROTHER AGAINST BROTHER

As we move forward in the book of Genesis, it also does not take long for sibling rivalry to manifest. Once humankind embraces sin, conflict is inevitable, and wars within families are the first of many tragic outcomes that will set the stage for perpetual war. In Genesis 4 we are introduced to Cain and Abel, the first children of Adam and Eve. We are told in verse 2 that Abel keeps flocks and Cain raises crops from the soil. In verses 3–7 we encounter this narrative:

> In the course of time Cain brought some of the fruits of the soil as an offering to the LORD. And Abel also brought an offering to the LORD—fat portions from some of the firstborn of his flock. The LORD looked with favor on Abel and his offering, but on Cain and his offering he did not look with favor. So Cain was very angry, and his face was downcast. Then the LORD said to Cain, "Why are you angry? Why is your face downcast? If you do what is right, will you not be accepted? But if you do not do what is right, sin is crouching at your door; it desires to have you, but you must rule over it."

If you are familiar with this story, you know what comes next. If you are unfamiliar with it, I encourage you to read the entire narrative in context. The spoiler is that Cain kills his brother Abel in a jealous rage, hides the body, plays innocent before God, gets called out by God, gets cursed, and ultimately receives mercy from God via a promise that he won't be killed by other people. Then he gets banished. The end. And you thought *your* kids had trouble getting along! The next time they bicker in the backseat, be thankful there aren't any rocks around. There is more to Cain's journey in the Bible, but obviously this is not a happy or a particularly satisfying aspect of the story. If we attempt to reconstruct the conflict, we are left with unanswered questions. For example, it is not clear why Abel was favored over Cain. In context it may not matter, but it does create an interesting scenario in which one party receives something and another does not, resulting in anger and jealousy. That is a theme we will see over and over again.

What we learn early in Scripture is that humans express their sin nature in a variety of ways. Sin as a construct always starts with humans disobeying God, but a key theme throughout Scripture is our inability to get along with each other. The Bible and just about every history book ever written records conflict after conflict after conflict. The parties involved in the process do matter, along with the cultural, political, economic, religious, and social elements. However, the story that keeps getting told is that humans will fight with anyone else, including an only sibling. This may sadden us when we think of the whole of human history, but we should certainly not be surprised.

If we embrace the concept that we are God's children (and we should), we must be comfortable with the full gamut of that idea. For example, whether or not we have children, most people are aware that children engage in conflict. As discussed in the first chapter, families can provide the arena for some major boxing matches (metaphorical and literal), and most people are familiar with the image of young siblings fighting in the backseat while the parent tries to maintain their patience and the ability to keep driving safely. We know the protests "He started it!" and "Tell her to stop touching me!" Unfortunately, an honest assessment of humanity reveals that this phraseology can very easily be applied to adults and is not the exclusive domain of immature youngsters.

The reality is that we have grown comfortable with this tension and conflict. Granted, "comfortable" may not be the most apt descriptor, as the word suggests that we find solace in the fights that occur at home and abroad. However, there is truth to the hypothesis that we have resigned ourselves to differences. There may also be credence to the idea that some humans (including Christians) live with a perpetual enemy complex. Scripture does tell us that there are true spiritual enemies and that Satan is real. However, many Christians take this perspective to a point at which they go looking for enemies, both at home and abroad. Some of this mindset stems from the sheer volume of anger, resentment, and ongoing strife that we see every single day. How can we not feel as though conflict is normal when we experience it on a weekly, daily, or even hourly basis? Is there any hope, or is this just the way humanity functions?

SOME THOUGHTS ON TERRITORY

Admittedly, this book should not be mistaken for a textbook, nor will I delve deeply into the intricacies of historical analysis. However, it is reasonable to suggest that conflict in the family of God has followed certain patterns over time. For example, let's talk about territory. The word *territory* can have several meanings. There is the geographic perspective, in which a territory is a plot of land with a defined (but movable) boundary. History tells us that borders are subject to change and that boundaries on a map are truthfully just arbitrary lines. As Psalm 86:9 reminds us, "All the nations you have made will come and worship before you, Lord; they will bring glory to your name." This verse is a statement of worship, but it is also a subtle reminder that those nations made by God can also be unmade in accordance with His will. In addition to our physical perspective on territory, there is the more conceptual version of the word, whereby territory is more generally about what someone owns or has jurisdiction over in a personal or organizational setting. An example might be a field of expertise, where someone might suggest that any questions about that area are the so-called territory of a certain individual.

It can be difficult to determine the origin of certain sayings, but suffice it to say that there is a quote about land that has been variously attributed to Mark Twain, Roy Rogers, and even Lex Luthor's father in the 2006 film *Superman Returns*. The quote in its various forms refers to the idea that people should acquire or protect their land because it is the only thing that is no longer being produced. There is a level of subtle humor to the quote, but for some people this idea is a serious aspect of their investing philosophy. For some individuals and organizations, land acquisition is a major part of their financial stability and legacy. That said, can we ever be "out" of land? It is reasonable to state that there is a finite amount of land on our pale blue dot but that there are large portions of it out there that are financially worthless? Is your territory really shrinking, or are you simply having to rethink its relative value?

A person's home is sometimes referred to as their castle, at least metaphorically. Some people have constructed dwelling places with castle-like architecture, perhaps to emphasize this idea. When we think about the aspects of the modern home, there are myriad ways in which the dwelling is protected. We start with locks on the doors and perhaps add an alarm system or a dog for security (and, in the latter instance, companionship). Some people supplement their security with a firearm or two . . . or many. A lower-level deterrent may be the sprinkler system with the motion sensor that scares away burglars and stray animals with a mighty blast of municipal water.

The point is that the average person wants to project a message with regard to the boundary of their territory that "None shall pass." This is my world, and you are just visiting. As Christians, we may understand the biblical truth that everything has been given to us by the grace of God, so that we shouldn't be selfish, greedy, or overly protective. However, that can be a hard reality for many of us. To be fair, these items of defense are certainly functional and may indeed provide levels of security and peace of mind. That said, is the modern dwelling place really equipped to ward off an attack from armed bandits? Could the average Western house withstand a small army of sword-wielding warriors? Hardly. Even people who own various weapons may be ill-trained or ill-equipped to use them in the heat of an attack.

There are practical and functional reasons to take some of these steps and ensure a level of physical safety in your life. We don't like the idea of a stranger inside our home, whether or not they are taking our stuff or hurting our loved ones. On a more philosophical level, we don't like the idea of strangers inside our heads, potentially violating our core ideas. Someone who challenges your ideas is the intellectual equivalent of a home-invasion robber. My place, my stuff, my territory. Not yours. This is not a new idea. History shows us time and time again that people, countries, and ideologies want to keep others out.

NOT ALL TERRITORY IS LAND-BASED

Not all territory, as we have seen, consists in physical land. If we think about the role that areas of human occupation have played throughout history, we are reminded that defense of personal space is a consistent theme. The physical piece of land is a tangible example of territory, but we can also dig a little deeper into the conceptual and less tangible version of the word. Each of us has a certain physical territory we occupy, which includes our carbon-based body and a subjective zone of comfort. When you think about the idea of human touch, we maintain a standard of comfort as to how close certain people can get to our physical body before we feel as though our personal territory has been infringed upon.

If you have ever attended a sexual harassment training session, you know that one of the concepts taught has to do with these personal "bubbles." The terminology may be different from training to training, but the principle is the same. There is an invisible bubble around each individual person. This bubble represents the comfort level people have with others getting physically close to them. Obviously, each person's bubble may be different and will likely vary depending on the relationship. Even people who have a level of comfort with each other may, at times, seek to keep their bubble free from other people—or even each other! If I go for a jog and come home all sweaty, no one in the house may be in the mood for a hug. In more serious situations, people can become very leery or even frightened when someone unfamiliar gets too close to them. This is when people think about defending themselves, including with violent actions.

Another version of personal territory is even more abstract and could be described as worldview, attitudes, beliefs, and perspective on the world. If you were wondering where all the land talk was going in this chapter, it is at this point that we narrow our focus to the ongoing subject of the book. When someone questions our ideas or views on a subject, we can sometimes feel as though we ourselves are under personal attack, even if the person who is challenging our beliefs is nowhere near our physical body. In essence, our mind, and subsequently the thoughts that reside in that mind, comprise a cerebral territory. We invite some to join us in that territory, but others must stay outside the boundary. People guard their physical dwelling places with fences, dogs, and cameras. We may guard our bodies with different types of armor, weapons, training in hand-to-hand combat, or the piercing sound of our cries for help. How do we defend our territory of beliefs? Again, if we look at history, people groups have fought not just for physical territory. They have fought for ideas, beliefs, and the preservation of ideology.

WHAT IS AN ARGUMENT?

The word *argument* is interesting on many levels. There is certainly the *argument* that the word can represent a conflict between two or more people. If two people get into a physical conflict, it may have started with a verbal argument that eventually eroded into fisticuffs. Whether or not there is physicality involved, saying that two people *got into* an argument typically means that there was a difference of opinion. In some cases, there may also be accompanying emotions that make the conflict a little more heated. I will address those elements in later chapters. To be fair, there is a broad spectrum in terms of how emotionally involved people get when expressing different opinions and the role this plays in the formation and development of an argument.

Two (or more) people can certainly engage in an argument that is simply an exchange of different opinions. An argument can be expressed as a calm dialogue whereby views are expressed and no one gets particularly offended. The reasons for this scenario may be many, but oftentimes this may stem from prior trust relationships or the fact that the subject at hand is not particularly personal or divisive in nature. This is once again a theme we will unpack later.

There is also the idea that an argument may not represent conflict at all. We also use the word to refer to a proposal. In other words, you might ask someone to make the argument that a new product should be purchased or that an organization should move in a different direction. In essence, you are saying to the person: *Convince me*. Certainly, that gets into a borderline situation in which conflict can almost immediately appear. After all, for every argument there may be a counter argument. However, this is one way to approach the idea of different perspectives. Some solicit more passion, but it may be valuable to cultivate a mindset whereby we are open to being convinced.

The point is that conflict, both now and in the past, has often stemmed from two sides that are attempting to reach an accord. That is the diplomatic way of describing what has too often been a dark and sordid history of human conquests. Unfortunately, in many cases throughout human history, one side has not been particularly interested in what the other side thinks, feels, or wants. When countries have invaded other countries, there are rarely niceties exchanged first. There may be a large psychological gap between an invading nation and the petty theological differences among church members, but some thematic questions are the same. Specifically, are people interested in the territory (physical and ideological) they are about the enter, or is this simply an invasion?

OBSERVATIONS FROM JAMES

James 4:1–3 asks, "What causes fights and quarrels among you? Don't they come from your desires that battle within you? You desire but do not have, so you kill. You covet but you cannot get what you want, so you quarrel and fight. You do not have because you do not ask God. When you ask, you do not receive, because you ask with wrong motives, that you may spend what you get on your pleasures."

Passion is a fascinating word. A person wo is described as passionate might be complimented in some situations. We are called, for example, to be passionate followers of Christ. Granted, there is the possibility that using the word *passion* in connection with our faith may contribute to our seeing our Christian walk as one emotional experience after another.

This is a valid concern, as we don't want our faith in Christ to simply be about how we feel, which can be fleeting. Much like a love relationship in earthly marriage, longevity is about feeling love for a person but also deciding to love them when the going gets tough. However, passion can also be interpreted as sustained dedication, which fits well with the scriptural description of following Christ.

Of course, James understood that passions collide, and there is also a Latin root to passion that has to do with suffering. One dictionary defines passion as "the state or capacity of being acted on by external agents or forces." What is interesting about this passage in James is the phrase "your desires that battle within you." It is easy for us to blame other people for conflicts, but James seems to suggest that in many cases we are the problem.

We want things and cannot have them, so we take out our frustration on others. This may be a more simplified perspective, but consider what the apostle Paul writes in Romans 7:15: "I do not understand what I do. For what I want to do I do not do, but what I hate I do." Historically, humans have fought with each other, but our greatest enemy is our own sinful nature.

WAR IN THE CHURCH

Dictators, evil rulers, and other bad actors in history are easy to blame for wars, death, and general mayhem. History has documented a long list of one territory invading another, which often results in retaliatory bloodshed and long-term hatred between people groups. For Christians, it would be nice if we could confidently state that division has never occurred in the church. It may be fair to suggest that churches have not physically invaded and set fire to other congregations, but there have been plenty of angry, painful splits. Hello, denominations.

Over time, many churches have decided to divide over various issues. And divide. And divide some more. As discussed, territory is far more than land. Today, the modern church is a complicated maze of division and denomination, filled with subgroups and branches that even scholars can have a hard time tracing. If you look at the history of the particularly Western church, you'll encounter a litany of painful separations. Some things that lead churches to split seem more significant in context, but other issues seem very trivial. There are even denominations and congregations that would have a hard time articulating why they broke away in the first place.

Ultimately, division is a sad testament to the inability of the church to stay unified and resolve differences when it comes to how people interpret the biblical guidelines for church structure. There are situations in which churches choose to merge, but we would prefer this to happen out of a desire for unity and not just because both congregations have declined over time and are just trying to survive with more warm bodies. In essence, a split congregation is a divorce—and the end of a sacred relationship among fellow believers. This is a tragedy, and the lingering frustration stems from individuals who are unable to even talk with each other about more than the most surface-level issues.

WE JUST DON'T GET ALONG, . . . BUT THERE IS HOPE!

We would do well to study human history and seek to understand how our sinful nature has been manifested. An oft-quoted phrase reminds us that "history repeats itself." This resonates with people, but it isn't always accurate. History incorporates *all* of the elements of change, including culture, technology, language, and ideology. Since everything is moving at once, it is hard to argue that our long-term timeline can be boiled down to basic themes. Despite that complexity, we can point to Scripture and suggest that "sinful human behavior repeats itself." That element has not changed. How sin manifests itself in society does change, however, and we will discuss that later in the book.

I know what some of you might be thinking at this point: this chapter was kind of a downer and doesn't offer a ton of hope for humanity. The reader might say, "Yeah, I get it. Humans don't get along. They never have, never well. The fall wrecked everything, and sin keeps us apart." To a certain extent that is true, but despite all the frustrating and depressing aspects of history, we have hope. Why? Because God is the same yesterday, today, and tomorrow. Christ is risen, He is risen indeed! The church is still the bride of Christ, and despite our unfaithfulness and fractured infrastructure the Holy Spirit is still working in our community. That is exciting.

In the next chapter I will talk about redemption; while we cannot overcome sin by our actions, we can pursue God's plan through the power of the Holy Spirit. Let's get to work.

PRACTICAL TIP

If you have some time and want an interesting project, list all of your material possessions. Yes, all of them. Every single item you own. Then think through how many of those objects you really need or would be sad if you were no longer to own.

DISCUSSION QUESTIONS

1. Do you think of your dwelling place as your castle, and what steps have you taken to defend it? Are there additional steps you would like to take?
2. How would you define your personal territory?
3. Are there perceived threats, either tangible or conceptual, that cause you to feel a need to mount a defense?
4. What are some subjects that have historically caused you to get into conflict with others?
5. Do you ever feel as though your beliefs are "under attack"? How do you deal with that feeling?

3

DESIRES FOR REDEMPTION

HONESTY CHECK

Do you believe that the world can be, for lack of a better word, "better"? Do you really want the world to be a better place? If so, do you want it to be better for everyone or just for certain people (or groups)?

Just for fun, let us assume that you have recently inherited or won a rather large sum of money. The dollar amount is not important for this fictional scenario, but for the sake of this example I will suggest that it is large enough that you, your children, and perhaps your grandchildren will have a sizable source of ongoing support moving forward. A happy day, hopefully. To keep this somewhat in perspective, I will add the caveat that you will maintain some semblance of a modest lifestyle, in accordance with the way you were raised. After all, you don't want money to change you, right? No fancy sports cars and mansions for you. The question for the moment is, Will you go to work today?

It may be somewhat problematic to compare eternal life with God to the situational change affected by the infusion of such an earthly dollar amount, but that is the analogy I will attempt to draw. Eternal life is priceless, and the good news is that Christ followers who have given their lives over to Him will receive just that incalculable reward. Happier day. Happier *life*! While this is amazing news, Christians can sometimes forget to celebrate; we can keep our petty problems in the forefront of our consciousness as we work through the complexities and distractions of a sinful world. So, now that I have reminded you of your invaluable eternal reward, are you going to work (in the kingdom) today?

GOT REDEMPTION?

Redemption is a complicated word. One dictionary defines redemption as "the action of saving or being saved from sin, error, or evil." As Christ followers, we have experienced redemption from sin through the blood and grace of Christ. Biblically, this is a one-time transaction, and if we subscribe to the belief that God is irresistible, we are good to go from a spiritual standpoint. Granted, there is a lot of theology to unpack around what salvation is and is not, but suffice it to say that we are blessed beyond measure by the redemption of the cross. That dictionary definition can also have earthly applications, and people apply it to various societal problems, both large and small. Another definition is "the action of regaining or gaining possession of something in exchange for payment or clearing a debt." This definition also has opportunities for spiritual and pragmatic application, as it references the idea that something that has been lost can be found again through effort and overcoming obstacles.

We use the word *redemption* in a variety of contexts. If you have a gift card, you can redeem that form of payment for goods and services. When a person has done something selfish, we might say that they have redeemed themselves by completing an act of selflessness later on. In a larger context, the question we must ask is whether we truly believe that redemption on a variety of levels is (a) possible and (b) worth the effort.

The 1994 film *Shawshank Redemption* follows a small group of men who are doing "hard time" in prison, starting in the late 1940s. While some characters come up for parole from time to time, the plot suggests that most of the inmates either have a life sentence or will be in prison long enough that the prospect of getting out is too far in the distance to be compelling. If you have ever talked with someone who has been sentenced to prison for many years, they will echo the sentiment that thinking about freedom can be discouraging if a potential release date is too far off in the future.

As Christians, we can draw a parallel between this mindset and our walk as Christ followers. This is not to suggest that we are discouraged felons locked in a prison, but we have been promised a heavenly reward that may be years (if not decades) away. In the meantime, how are we going to live our life? The two main characters in *Shawshank Redemption* each utters an identical line at different points in the story. The line goes, "Get busy living or get busy dying." The context in each case is very important, but the meaning can have multiple applications. We have all encountered a variety of people in life, including individuals who have spent time in prison. Sadly, some people go into prison angry, and the environment of incarceration only serves to amplify their personal darkness. Other people decide that they are going to be as productive as possible, and they focus on reading, correspondence, meaningful work, and self-improvement. Their stories are inspiring.

Are you busy living—or, if you are honest, are you busy dying? That may seem like one of those obvious questions that a preacher asks from the pulpit. The preacher asks, "Do you love Jesus?" The congregation nods. The preacher then says, "Are you going to go out and live out the Great Commission?" The congregation nods again (with a few low-energy utterances of "Amen"). What I am getting at is the idea that grace, while amazing, can be taken for granted. We may not come out and say it, but our actions (or lack thereof) can sometimes suggest that we do not feel a call to action, fueled by gratitude. We are saved, and the world is welcome to join us if others wish, but the important thing is that *I* am assured of salvation. Again, this may seem like a selfish premise that no one would actually believe or utter. And yet, if we are again honest (there is that word *again*), we are still sinners. We are a selfish lot.

DO YOU BELIEVE IN MIRACLES?

If you are a hockey fan and I use the phrase "miracle on ice," chances are you know of which I speak. Even many non-hockey fans may know this reference. This phrase refers to the 1980 Winter Olympics and an improbable win by the United States hockey team. The backstory is that the hockey team from the Soviet Union had been a powerhouse for many years. Prior to the 1980 Olympics, the U.S. hired a successful college coach who employed a new style of roster selection and strategy on the ice. The young, hungry team faced heavy odds, overcame obstacles, and eventually toppled the mighty Soviet team before going on to win the gold medal. The legendary sportscaster Al Michaels was the play-by-play voice for this memorable back-and-forth game, and his high-energy description of the action in the final minutes reached a climax with the now-legendary phrase "Do you believe in miracles?!?" If you love movies, the 2004 chronicle of this story (aptly titled *Miracle*) is very good and even includes spliced audio by Michaels.

Do *you* believe in miracles? Yes, that is a serious question I am asking. Do you believe in the power of God to change the world, to redeem, to bring about glimpses of kingdom here on Earth? If you are looking for the key question in this chapter, this is it. Do. You. Believe. In. Miracles? If so, are you willing to get up today and serve, be challenged, look for opportunities to love hurting people, pursue difficult conversations with your family and friends, and seek out God's will? Again, I am throwing out the obvious questions that are asked by preachers somewhere just about every Sunday. Based on the argument that the church has sometimes been less than enthusiastic about belief in miracles, this needs to be asked again. And again. And perhaps just one more time.

At this point in the process, I need to drop in a reminder about the Holy Spirit (just in case you forgot). Even in the church there is a lot of "I" and "we" language. We talk about our plans and visions and what we are going to accomplish together. Churches write mission statements and strategic plans, followed by celebrations when they meet their budget and reach their yearly goals. This is not wholly wrong, but we must always be cognizant of worldly language and mindsets that may creep into our thinking. God is in control. The Holy Spirit and not our own efforts will be changing hearts and minds. Yes, we can have a mindset of redemption, but, ultimately, we must continue to pray for guidance, wisdom, energy, and perseverance. Our efforts and attitudes are fleeting. We may believe in miracles for the moment, but, much as with shiny objects, we are quickly and easily distracted.

I DON'T KNOW WHY YOU BOTHER

This is a phrase you may have heard from time to time, either directed at yourself or in reference to some particularly difficult task. The phrase suggests that effort was, is, or will be directed toward a challenge that either cannot be overcome or isn't worth the effort. Often, the phrase refers to a quest the speaker believes will almost certainly result in failure. In some cases, the quest at hand is related to one person trying to convince another on a subject on which there seems to be little flexibility of belief.

To be fair, there is some merit to this concern, and it is the counterbalance or offset to a redemptive mindset. Life, in many contexts, is a paradox. We are called to redeem a fallen world through the power of the Holy Spirit, but we are constantly distracted, discouraged, and derailed. Sin and brokenness just keep coming, and for every step forward it can seem as though we take two steps backward. Lest you think I am letting you off the hook, I don't state that as a justification for giving up. We simply need to acknowledge that, because of sin, we can be prone to weakness. All our efforts may result in measurable earthly failure. Therefore, the church, while its functionality can be frustrating at times, is a vital gathering space for encouragement and accountability. We must remain focused on the big picture.

I have spent a little time on social media, which I will touch on again in chapter 11. For better or worse, I have engaged in a variety of political, social, and theological discussions. Some online dialogues have been respectful and productive. Others have quickly gone off the rails and devolved into a contentious stream of back-and-forth aggravation. A quote I once posted claims that "there are moments when I feel like people don't really want the world to be as they describe. Blaming others is too often a reason given for a lack of measurable progress. Perhaps dialogue, learning how others experience life, and nuanced thinking are too much of a daily challenge. Despite evidence to the contrary, I remain hopeful that we are capable and willing to work through our differences, find commonality, and pursue thoughtful solutions to complex societal puzzles."

This is our paradox. Do we believe that the world can be redeemed, or are we content as Christians to ride out our days, mix in a few moments of community outreach, and wait for eternal life with God? I will admit that there are times when I don't really feel like working. Because I've grown up in a country that has allowed me a good deal of material privilege, it is easy for me to get comfortable with leisure and excess. I've had some wonderful opportunities to go on trips, see sights, and spend quality time with family and friends in scenic locations. I enjoy good food and good conversation, and I look forward to stepping away from the so-called responsibilities of the world. This prospect can be very appealing, and it is easy to convince myself that I have done enough to advance the gospel and love for other people that I now "deserve" some rest and relaxation. The problem is that . . . I don't. There is always work to be done. An understanding of Sabbath is one thing, but a Sabbath reprieve isn't time away from kingdom work so much as it is time to commune with God and recharge before continuing our call to evangelism and redemption.

What we also must keep in mind is that we are prone to surrounding ourselves with people who think as we do. In chapter 8 I will talk about echo chambers and the challenge of (sometimes) escaping a shared mindset. It is easy to find a group of people who affirm your beliefs, including the idea that *those other* people are wrong and that the world will be a better place once they figure out how wrong they are. Too often our redemption mindset includes a belief that we have done all we can and that real change will happen only when *other* people figure out they are misguided. Unfortunately, the feeling is often mutual.

WHAT CAN WE REALLY GET DONE?

Time for a reality check. Despite our best efforts, the world is still sinful. In the words of John in Revelation 21:1, "Then I saw 'a new heaven and a new earth,' for the first heaven and the first earth had passed away, and there was no longer any sea." What that verse does not say is "and the people didst smile, for they had overcome the world through their good work and therefore fixed everything." Only God will bring about a new heaven and a new earth. We are called to keep working, but we must remember that we should measure our success in obedience and response to calling, not in earthly accomplishment.

With that I must drop in the discouraging reminder that *we* aren't going to get to our desired destination. As of the writing of this book, I live in Southern California, and there is an island off the coast called Catalina. You can see it on clear days, and many enjoy it as a tourist destination after a reasonable boat ride. I once heard a pastor use Catalina as an example of our efforts to overcome sin and redeem the world. If you were to run your hardest off the end of the pier toward Catalina before jumping, you would sadly not reach it. The island is 31 miles away. Physics alone will deny your efforts. If you recruit the best long jumper in the world to attempt the same feat, chances are they will get farther out in the water than you did. No disrespect to your jumping ability, . . . but come on. The pragmatic and theological reality is that in the grand scheme that person may be closer to the island but is still hopelessly far away.

That may seem as though I am giving up and that the premise of this whole book is invalid. The difficulty with balancing hope and so-called realism is that we aren't sure of the point at which unlimited possibility transitions into practical application. This is a paradox every day of our life. We can achieve more. We can push ourselves beyond our normal boundaries. Great things can happen when people gather and lay their burdens at the foot of the cross. The question is, Will we make those choices daily? Will we get up every day and strive to redeem a fallen world? Will our efforts be sustained and tenacious?

Again, I am not just talking about a pep talk that is intended to get you moving, though that is a part of it. In 1991 the long-running comedy show *Saturday Night Live* debuted a new sketch called "Daily Affirmations with Stuart Smalley." The Smalley character, played by comedian and eventual United States Senator Al Franken, was a seemingly insecure individual who employed several self-help mechanisms and catch-phrases to deal with his burdensome life. His most famous phrase, typically said into a mirror, was, "I'm good enough, I'm smart enough, and doggone it, people like me."

I am not recommending that awkward conversations in the church and their connection to redemption of the world start and end with positive self-talk. Certainly, there is value in reminding ourselves of what God has given us. However, I feel a need to constantly remind you, the reader, that I am not writing a self-help book. The world is filled with cognitive mechanisms that focus on the ability and drive of the individual to overcome just about anything. These mechanisms can be valuable, and we should not shy away from them, but daily we should pray with humility as we lay our burdens before our Lord. As mentioned, we must focus our efforts on sustained obedience to the calling of redemption, not on what we think we can accomplish in our short earthly life.

THE LONG GAME (OR PERHAPS VERY SHORT)

I mentioned earlier in the chapter that our sense of urgency may not be heightened if we assume that we will be around for decades. We may indeed live our whole lives without Christ returning. However, Christ could return today. Plus, the Holy Spirit is already here. What we must face is our own sense of urgency and willingness to work toward certain outcomes. Are you willing to invest in tangible, earthly projects that may or may not bear fruit until after you are gone? An ecologically-minded individual might think about this through the lens of investment in alternative energies or exploration of the cosmos. A person who lives in the moment may have a hard time putting time, energy, and money into those endeavors once they realize the pace of innovation is relatively slow. We might not have flying cars, energy independence, or a colony on Mars during our lifetimes, . . . and that is okay.

Despite the relative shortness of human life, there are distinct stages that can impact our thinking about urgency, legacy, and how we are to order our day-to-day life. When you are a child, you can't wait to be an adult so that you can have greater control over your life choices. Arrival at so-called adulthood can be an overrated experience in that you have choices, but also the understanding of their relative weight and significance. As people age, they may lament how fast their life has gone by and what they weren't able to accomplish. Without spending time unpacking the plot, the classic Christmas film *It's a Wonderful Life* includes an understated line from an exasperated character who proclaims, "Oh . . . youth is wasted on the wrong people!" As Christians, we should live our lives as though Christ will be returning tomorrow, but at the same time be willing to put effort into conversations and initiatives that might take a very long time to unfold.

I mentioned different life stages, but for a moment let us focus on one group of people, particularly since the American church tends to be populated by an older group of attendees. Retirement is a construct that often refers to employment, and for those with means it can be a time to rest after many years of service in a particular vocation. Granted, many cultures have different perspectives on retirement and on how an older population fits into the broader society. The more complicated and pertinent question of retirement applies to our spiritual walk and our role in the church. You may have heard individuals verbalize that they have put in their time and no longer must serve in certain capacities. There are some reasonable aspects of altering our service based on age and physical ability. However, our service to the kingdom never ends. Earthly retirement is not necessarily a biblical idea, particularly in terms of redeeming a kingdom. If anything, this life season might afford even more time to dialogue and learn. Instead of retirement, there needs to be a mindset of *reassignment* while still pursuing redemption.

PUTTING CONFLICT IN CONTEXT

We do understand that dialogue on complex topics can be awkward, that seeking to redeem societal problems can seem daunting, and that there may be hesitancy to address issues that are going to require a lot of prolonged interaction. However, we are still talking about conversational challenges that, in the grand scheme of life, the universe, and everything else that exists, are far less epic than the difficulties some people face every day. To be fair, we must not minimize the impact of awkward conversations because there can be relational loss through dialogue. We can be bold, but we must also be savvy.

It is also important to keep in mind that, as a Christian, you are supposed to be running around telling people about this person named Jesus who was *dead* and then came back to life. You do realize that, at face value, that sounds a little strange to an outsider, right? Despite that seemingly outlandish claim, it is the core of our faith. With that in mind, you're going to tell me that, though you are willing to sell that dubious story to a skeptical public, resolving a little theological or political dispute with your fellow church member is not worth the effort?

Despite the challenges, this is our calling. We are commanded in Scripture to pursue the Great Commission. Matthew 28:19–20 quotes Jesus as saying, "Go therefore and make disciples of all nations, baptizing them in the name of the Father and of the Son and of the Holy Spirit, and teaching them to obey everything I have commanded you. And surely I am with you always, to the very end of the age." It may be a theological stretch to suggest that dialogue is implied in this passage, but as I will discuss in the next chapter, conversation encompasses myriad audiences. Verse 19 calls for the disciples to teach, and in our modern age some of the best teachers are those who can engage their audience in a collaborative discussion that encourages learning for both the so-called sage on the stage and the students in the audience.

WHAT PIRATES TEACH US

Let me close with perhaps an unorthodox example from the 2003 movie *Pirates of the Caribbean: The Curse of the Black Pearl*. Partway through the film (spoiler alert), protagonist Captain Jack Sparrow is marooned on a deserted island by the villainous antagonist Captain Hector Barbossa. Jack promptly escapes the island, tracks down his rival, and subtly saunters into a meeting between Barbossa and his crew. Barbossa looks incredulously at Jack and says, "It's not possible." Jack cleverly corrects him with the witty, but also wise phrase, "Not probable."

Because of our unbelief, we can struggle to believe that redemption is possible. As Captain Jack reminded us, redemption may not be probable, but too often that recognition is our self-doubt and sinful nature talking. Do we have faith, or not? We ask everyone else to take a leap of faith, but what about us? As Paul declares in Philippians 4:13, "I can do all [things] through him who gives me strength." *All* things. That applies to each of us as well, and it is exciting! As a final note, I encourage you not to focus on the "I" in that verse. Focusing on "through him" is a much better daily goal. Redemption, anyone?

PRACTICAL TIP

Make a list of realities in your own life or in the larger world that are "better" than they used to be. Or make a list of "redemption" stories that are about people, places, or things.

DISCUSSION QUESTIONS

1. If you are honest, do you believe that absolutely anything is possible? Or does your practical thinking prevent this type of openness?
2. What actions do you pursue daily that indicate your belief that God can redeem this world?
3. Are you concerned about your legacy? Do you find yourself avoiding certain causes, initiatives, or projects because you aren't certain they can be accomplished in your lifetime?
4. If you desired to capture your attitude toward redemption on your tombstone, what would you like it to say?

4

THE BELIEF IN DIALOGUE

HONESTY TIME

Is world peace possible? If so, what will it take to achieve that goal? If not, how do you know when dialogue should be abandoned?

Let's get together one of these days. Time for you and me to have a one-on-one. This needs to be a face-to-face conversation. Is there a time when you and I can get together soon? Let's sit down together for a heart-to-heart. Time for an intervention. We are going to have a come-to-Jesus meeting. Let's talk. Do you have time to grab a coffee sometime soon? Please stop by my office today. One of these days we should have a chat. Can we talk?

What do all these phrases have in common? They all refer to the basic premise that in life there are problems and that those issues are often going to be addressed through dialogue. Admittedly, some of these expressions/invitations may indicate little more than a desire to get together. There does not have to be interpersonal conflict for people to gather and enjoy good conversation and a valued relationship. After all, humans remain social creatures who connect via in-person experiences. Does dialogue always work? No. Do we continue to utilize this complex form of human communication? Yes. Let us discuss why that is.

AVOIDING PISTOLS AT DAWN

Admittedly, we could just engage in a physical fight instead of talking things out. Rather than suggesting a hearty dialogue, we could always say, "You and I haven't been getting along lately. What do you say we set a time to meet and pummel each other until one of us relents?" This is not something to be proud of, but humans are pretty good at physical violence. We get into everything from one-on-one fistfights to wars that encompass large sections of world geography. Humans are great at creating mayhem. Unfortunately, we can get into these scuffles very quickly, and once a fight starts it can be hard to break up. If you have ever watched a hockey game, you know that fighting is part of the experience. Sometimes the referees will jump in and separate players immediately, but at other times they let them go for a time and break up the fight only after the players are getting too tired to keep going. If only we could trust humanity to tire of fighting. So far that has yet to occur.

It is interesting that we human beings like to observe our friends in the animal kingdom. How many television shows and documentaries are there about creatures that roam the land and glide through the sea? In particular, we love video clips of animals fighting. The raw energy of nature makes for good television. In general, we humans consider ourselves to be higher beings, and in many ways we are. However, history is littered with horrifying, gut-wrenching periods of slaughter, hatred, and prolonged aggression. Why does this keep happening? Are we simply violent individuals who must regularly take out our aggressions on somebody else? Unfortunately, the answer appears to be yes. Sin remains.

The reasons for conflict are many, but, ultimately, we experience fights (verbal and otherwise) when conflicting beliefs cannot comfortably coexist. Take some diverse viewpoints, some impatience, mix in some hatred, and *boom* (no pun intended), you have a war. A particularly disturbing aspect of human conflict is a construct we have come to define as genocide. When genocide occurs, one group attempts to wipe out another group in its entirely. This is the ultimate example of people losing all hope for dialogue, or even for coexisting. The horror of genocide is that it can include *all* the people in the targeted group, including children. For obvious reasons, we focus on the loss of life when genocide occurs. What we must keep in mind, however, is that genocide is also about killing culture. Genocide kills ideas, worldviews, and beliefs. It is devastating to watch or study this phenomenon, but it should spur us on to dialogue. Unfortunately, humans will sometimes approach our inability to communicate in the worst possible ways.

It might go without saying that we are trying to avoid violence in our fragile world, but just for the sake of checking off boxes let me directly state that we should try to avoid violence. Period. There, I have done my due diligence. Granted, not everyone feels that violence must be dismissed as a prospective solution, or at least avoided at all costs. This is a complicated subject for Christians, who read about conflict in the Bible and wonder when it is appropriate to invade a country, execute an individual who has committed heinous crimes against humanity, or defend loved ones with violent methodologies. We can talk about that. Yes, talk.

FRIEND OR FOE?

If you have ever found yourself wandering into an auto dealership in search of your next vehicle, you may be familiar with the friendly salesperson who quickly heads your way. There are smiles, handshakes, inquiries about your name, and the general pleasantries that typically accompany two people meeting for the first time. Of course, this is not just a friendly meet-and-greet. Most people will walk through the motion of pleasant conversation in this situation, but what if they didn't? What if, instead of playing along, you were to say, "Look, can we dispense with the chit-chat? I know why I am here. You know why I am here. Let the games begin!"

Maybe that sounds a little harsh, but there are situations in which dialogue is not built around collaborative solutions and enhancing relationships. If anything, some conversations are specifically built around competition. Or, more generally, there is a broad understanding that two opposing forces are coming to the table and that both sides will likely be preparing for battle. Unless your child is an absolute angel (unlikely) or they are good at hiding their sins (more likely), there will come a point when you as a parent will tell them that the two of you need to sit down and "have a talk." These are not moments parents relish.

If you have ever asked a moody teenager to sit down and explain their behavior, you know that this is not necessarily a welcome exchange. The child may not be your enemy per se, but they certainly aren't excited to discuss life with you. Oftentimes they know a lecture or rebuke is coming. The same could be said for many conversations in the church that focus on theology, politics, and social issues. People avoid these topics (and thinkers of a different mindset) because the interaction is going to entail too much work. Why clutter life with conversations that won't end with warmth and shared belief?

Granted, our perspective on relative roles in dialogue can change depending on how topics are approached, and we will discuss that later in the book. On a personal and societal level, we often justify violence or an aggressive approach when we are attacked first. In situations of conflicting dialogue, we often have the same attitude. The so-called "they started it" phrase appears in childhood and evolves (or devolves) into adulthood. It is certainly fair and just for us to defend our worldview, particularly when we are directly confronted. However, we must keep our goal in mind. Do we simply want to defend our territory (chapter 2) and resist our attacker, or can we find a way to help the aggressor see the value of our perspective?

GETTING THE POINT ACROSS

Language and other forms of communication are fascinating aspects of the human experience. In a vast array of settings, commonly understood concepts are a constant pursuit. When two people who do not speak the same language need to engage in some sort of dialogue or transaction, they may utilize a whole host of methodologies to establish links of understanding. This may include hand gestures, expressions, pointing, attempting to say words from the other person's language, and drawing pictures. Unfortunately, we can also resort to talking more slowly or loudly. Talking more slowly may help in some situations when there is some shared understanding of language, but talking louder may actually work against understanding. The same challenges exist for people who speak the *same* language. Raising our voice rarely helps the situation, and in some cases this can escalate the conflict.

Charades has been a popular game for a very long time, but it can also be a challenge for all involved. In Charades, a person is given a word that they must act out for their teammates, but they are not allowed to speak. They can use gestures and are allowed to make various motions to their teammates if the line of guessing is on the right track, but sometimes this fails to get the point across. If you have watched or participated in this or a similar game, you know that it can be highly entertaining but also frustrating. After all, you have this highly specialized language that you have spent your whole life developing. Why not use it? The reality is that even when people use all the words at their disposal, there can still be a breakdown in communication. Despite the hurdles, language and dialogue are often the best methodology we have. As mentioned, we prefer to keep talking rather than always turning to bloodshed.

The Socratic Method, or what some will categorize as a Socratic Seminar, is an oft-used conversational mechanism that educators and other facilitators will utilize to address complex issues. The method starts with a topic and asks for a perspective on that topic. The facilitator then asks a series of questions, which mostly focus on the origin of the perspective. A skilled facilitator asks a lot of *why* questions, along with asking about alternative viewpoints and the implications of an original perspective. This process can take some time, and it can be very helpful if the person answering the questions understands the depth and breadth of their own worldview. We will discuss that challenge in chapter 5.

Some individuals very much enjoy a robust Socratic Seminar, while others become frustrated if the questions do not result in resolution or end up going in circles. If we look at everything from our day-to-day dialogue to complex international diplomacy, we will recognize that we all use a form of this methodology. The goal is both shared understanding and mapping out a path forward. We will discuss this more in depth throughout the rest of the book, but at this point we can acknowledge that dialogue of this type attempts to establish defined beliefs, implications, and what can be done to find appropriate intersections.

A WORD ON CULTURE

Let me pause for a moment and offer a caveat about culture. We truly understand only our own culture. Period. Certainly, we can visit places, read books, watch movies, and have individuals tell us stories about growing up or living for an extended period in another part of the world. But don't kid yourself. These are glimpses, and brief looks at that. Also, keep in mind that just because you have experienced something similar to what someone else has does not mean that you have processed the same thoughts, emotions, and memories. True empathy, as a construct, is extremely difficult to achieve, if it is truly possible at all.

In Western society we are often unaware of the reality that some cultures simply do not dialogue. As in, certain topics are not discussed. Ever. *Ever!* Also, we can sometimes forget (or remain continually unaware) that ideas do not always translate easily from culture to culture. If you have studied language on any level, you know that certain words have easy equivalents. Picture this conversation:

Person 1: What is the word for ____________?
Person 2: It is ____________.
Person 1: (Repeats word, with or without the proper accent). Good to know.
Person 1 (again): What is the word for ____________?
Person 2: There isn't really a word for ____________.
Person 1: Why not?
Person 2: Because people don't just speak using different-sounding words; they also think differently.

When I talk about dialogue, I recognize that it is not as simple as sitting down and chatting. Some topics are tacitly off limit. Some families do not discuss anything. Ever.

I am a Western thinker, born and raised in a country that is very comfortable putting awkward topics on the table. Our country does many things well, but sometimes discretion is not one of them. I will address some of these nuances in the next chapter. Cultural differences can apply even to regional thinking. For example, I live and work in California, but it is always interesting to talk with non-Californians who in some cases view my state with both fascination and fear. There can be interesting, nuanced differences in the perspectives of thinkers from around the country, not to mention the world.

A TIME TO . . . NOT TALK?

As much as this book is built around a core belief that dialogue is a positive and productive means of resolving conflict and establishing a more robust community, there are limits. I will talk about this more in chapter 12, but there are situations in which humans are unyielding. The images that come to mind are of an unstoppable force and an immovable object. Or, more accurately, we can visualize the simple dynamic of two immovable objects, neither of which has any intention of yielding. To be fair, there is a fine line between stubbornness and conviction. Being comfortable with a thoughtful, introspective worldview does not mean that dialogue will not be entertained.

In addition, we must remember that dialogue may be a good solution, but perhaps not right now. There are times to actively listen (addressed in chapter 7), and there are also times to appropriately pause. It is probably inaccurate to suggest that time heals all wounds because some injuries do not simply get better without some sort of treatment. People are often the same way. There are situations in which time allows people to think, reestablish a different perspective, and infuse some feelings of calm. However, gaps of time do not solve all problems because unaddressed issues can quickly resurface.

There is also the issue of effort, of whether dialogue is worth the long-term benefit of mutual understanding. This will be addressed in various ways throughout the book, and we can draw inspiration from Matthew 7:6, in which Jesus says, "Do not give dogs what is sacred; do not throw your pearls to pigs. If you do, they may trample them under their feet, and turn and tear you to pieces." This Scripture is about the challenges of sharing the gospel message with a fiercely closed mind, but we can also apply the construct to a variety of situations in which dialogue occurs around complex subjects.

We must also acknowledge that dialogue does not always result in action or implementation. Humans are famous (or infamous) for making grand plans that look wonderful on paper but never manifest as measurable change. Granted, there is always a balance between talking things through and exploring the possible ramifications of direct measures. In the movie *The Bourne Identity*, two government officials are arguing about what to do about a rogue operative who has continued to elude them. One official says, "Well, so far, you've given me nothing but a trail of collateral damage from Zurich to Paris. I don't think I could do much worse." The other official responds with, "Well, why don't you go upstairs and book a conference room. Maybe you can talk him to death."

In his book *The Righteous Mind: Why Good People Are Divided by Politics and Religion*, author Jonathan Haidt suggests that people may have an overdeveloped belief that humans are capable of being rational creatures. There may be some wisdom to this perspective, particularly when we merge that mindset with an understanding of our sin nature. However, as Christians we must always remember the power of the Holy Spirit and remind ourselves daily that with God all things are possible.

WHO WOULD LIKE TO START?

In major college and professional sports where there is a television audience, there is often a post-game press conference where the coach or players will be asked about the game by a pool of reporters. Questions are typically asked about certain players, coaching decisions, opponents, mindsets, and key plays. The answers often feel as though they have been drawn from a list of predetermined press conference responses. From time to time there appear to be moments of transparency, but one can also conclude that true feelings are being hidden.

When members of a church community gather, there may be a similar outcome. Think about the conversations that can occur after a worship service. Do people jump right into a discussion of a sermon or other complicated topics? Are we willing to ask questions and express different viewpoints? Or when someone starts a conversation by asking how another person is doing, do they really want to know, and does the person being asked feel free to answer honestly? Or is it just simpler to exit a church building, talk about sports and the weather, and hide our true feelings from people we may or may not fully trust?

Ultimately, many people acknowledge the worth of dialogue, but few want to engage in awkward conversations. Some of this is understandable. Who of us gets up in the morning and says, "I sure hope I can have an awkward, complicated discussion with a friend or family member today! When I have that conversation, I also hope it puts a strain on our relationship and makes it difficult for us to maintain the status quo of our relationship status." While some individuals do enjoy a robust discussion on difficult topics, many others must be encouraged to participate. Or people wait for just the right moment, which in some cases will never come because the parameters for ideal discussion do not emerge. People can always come up with a reason to engage in a difficult discussion *later on*.

THIS IS GOING TO TAKE SOME WORK

Let us close with a couple of key points. The first is that dialogue requires more than one person to be involved. There are elements of speaking in the process, but there is also listening, which I will address in chapter 7. The second point is that both parties must acknowledge that they have something to learn. That is a big step for some people, and it requires a level of humility. Whether or not they admit it, some people believe they have an answer for just about everything. Or they have an answer for all the subjects that interest them, which manifests as topics that meet a singular requirement in terms of importance.

As I have already stressed several times, honesty is helpful. Therefore, I must be honest again at this juncture. A belief in dialogue does not mean I would ever suggest that the process is easy. Far from it. Dialogue is work, and efforts can take time, resiliency, and patience. Some conversations make progress, while, unfortunately, other dialogue seems to go in a regressive direction. It is easy to get discouraged. After a difficult conversation, we can quickly think or utter the phrase, "See, I told you it wouldn't work." Despite that, I will continue to encourage discussion. It may be slow, frustrating, and painstaking at times. For most life situations, however, awkward conversations are still preferable to a pair of pistols at dawn.

There are a couple of items worth mentioning when it comes to putting in the work. Admittedly, there are plenty of conversations that happen daily, and most people are willing to engage with each other on a base level. The question is often whether individuals are willing to overcome obstacles to achieve a desirable outcome. The phrase "agree to disagree" is reasonably common, but there exists the possibility that we may at times jump to this construct too quickly. Therefore, the person who acknowledges the worth of dialogue must engage in self-evaluation with regard to their level of commitment. In other words, do we have the grit to try something more than once? Are we willing to keep dialoguing with a person even though every conversation seems to end up at the same place?

KEEP AT IT

We will end with an anecdote of hope and a reminder that dialogue does not mean an abandonment of viewpoint. Dialogue is a wonderful tool, but outcomes will vary. Not so long ago there was a Little League World Series on television. We should note that these are young players, and whether they should feel the pressure of being televised is debatable, but society loves competition and a good story. During the game a batter stands in the box waiting for the pitch. Unfortunately, the next thrown ball gets away from the pitcher and, rather than traveling over the plate, sails high and hits the batter in the helmet. The batter goes down, clutching his head. Everyone gasps. Coaches and medical personnel rush to his aid. After a few tense minutes, they establish that the player is okay, and he walks to first base while the crowd gives him a standing ovation.

Meanwhile, the pitcher is overcome with guilt and emotion. Sports is an interesting forum for competition because the core goal is to defeat your opponent. Coaches often teach an attitude of competition, and some will preach a mindset of steely resolve when it comes to how the game is approached. Some even use the phraseology "no mercy." The hit batter could easily have become angry and used the incident to fuel the fires of competitive resolve by yelling at the pitcher as he walked to first base. Instead, the hit batter quietly walked to first and, after evaluating the situation, saw that his opponent was hurting (emotionally). Even competitive athletes can experience remorse and compassion when their actions cause real physical pain and the possibility of permanent damage. The batter left the base, walked to the pitcher's mound, put his arms around the player, and appeared to assure him that he was okay. The two were soon joined by the pitcher's teammates, who all patted the batter on the back and expressed their happiness that he wasn't seriously injured.

That kind of account gives us hope. It was a tender moment and a reminder that, even in a competitive sports environment, players can acknowledge the more important issues of life. Keep in mind that the game did go on. There were a winner and a loser, and likely some disappointment afterward. However, there was still a sense of a bigger picture, and in this case the wisdom was provided by children. It is easy in a competitive world to brush off a hurt or weaker opponent, even if the dispute is in the form of a simple conversation. We aren't suggesting that you should hug every person after a heated conversation, but then again, maybe we should follow the example of these youngsters. Why are we here but to continue looking for ways to love each other and coexist is a fallen world? At minimum, we should always seek to say "Let's talk again."

PRACTICAL TIP

Make a list of people with whom you talk on a regular basis. They may be friends, family, or coworkers, but is there anything else they have in common? Now make a list of people with whom you would hesitate to meet for coffee or a beer. Why are those people on the list, and what does that group have in common?

DISCUSSION QUESTIONS

1. Should dialogue always be the goal, or are there times when it should be abandoned? If so, when?
2. Why do humans struggle to establish productive dialogue?
3. How good are you with pursuing dialogue when you do not agree with a person?
4. Are there particular individuals with whom you struggle to dialogue? If so, why?
5. What is the hardest part of either deciding to talk or engaging in a difficult conversation?

5

CONFRONTING BIASES AND LIMITATIONS

HONESTY CHECK

What are your biases, and are you able to articulate them?

Years ago a student walked into my class. As a fan of professional baseball, I immediately recognized his hat as belonging to the Baltimore Orioles. "Orioles fan?" I asked. The student looked at me blankly, before responding with the always-articulate response "What?" Thinking he didn't hear me, I repeated the question and asked, "Are you an Orioles fan?" The blank look on his face remained unchanged. At this point I came to the profound conclusion that he may not have been a baseball fan. I said, "Your hat is worn by the Baltimore Orioles baseball team." The student took the hat off, looked at it for a moment, shrugged, and said, "Oh, I just liked the bird."

I assumed. It turns out I was wrong. Did I commit a moral crime and trespass on the civil rights of this individual by lumping him in with all the loyal Baltimore fans who enjoy the team? Not exactly. At face value you might suggest that this was an understandable and innocent error. No real harm done. However, I did stereotype this individual by linking a visual cue with the closed membership of a particular subset of society. Assumptions can be innocent but still wrong, hurtful, and damaging.

Stereotypes are easy to establish. Start by reading about or hearing a judgment regarding a particular group. Encounter one (yes, just one) example of this, which you may or may not have conditioned yourself to detect. Just like that, the stereotype is born. You might ask whether people are willing to make broad-based assessments and worldview decisions based on such a small dataset. Yes, they are. It happens much more often than you might think. Welcome to bias, our go-to filter for data collection, evaluation, and decision-making.

Again, let's do a little soul searching and transparent admitting of our character flaws. I am biased and prejudiced. Also, I don't know everything. These may not be earth-shattering admissions, but they are important statements, nonetheless. Also, you are biased. In addition, you also do not know everything. This should not be a surprise to you. If you do not believe that you are biased, may I suggest some self-reflection and perhaps a round of feedback from people who know you in different societal contexts. A resistance to the idea that we are biased is understandable. After all, we prefer to think of ourselves as open-minded, tolerant, and willing to accept a host of humans and their associated beliefs.

There are certainly people who admit their depravity. In fact, some people exhibit so much self-loathing that they have a hard time accepting the amazing gift of grace that God provides. On the flipside, there are plenty of individuals who do not struggle at all with loving themselves. For many of those people (me included), the idea that they are a bad person is not the most pleasant thought. A Christ follower can recognize that they have some flaws due to sin, but the idea that we are unable to accept other people is a little harder to swallow. The word *prejudice* is very powerful, and we don't love to self-apply that label.

NORMAL IS NOT NORMAL

As humans, we use the word normal as though it were an objective, measurable quantity. There are cultures, settings, and environments that have established agreed-upon benchmarks for behaviors and expectations. In other words, groups of people will sometimes agree on what they judge to be normal. However, the construct is still elusive in many ways. It is perhaps more accurate to suggest that normality is a singular perspective, which can change at any time. Is common sense truly common? No. It never has been.

I was born and raised in the American city of Seattle, a member of a Christian family that also consisted of two loving parents and a pair of sisters. I have watched baseball, football, and basketball since I was a child, and hamburgers have been part of my meal rotation throughout my life. These are random facts about me, but they represent part of my so-called normal. Had I been raised in a different part of the world, it is quite possible that every one of these variables could have been vastly different.

Earlier in this chapter, I mentioned the innocence of assumption. Admittedly, many people do not go out of their way to be hateful and exact prejudicial judgments on others. I assume that people wearing hats from sports teams are fans. That is part of my bias, and it would not be difficult to find data that supports the supposition that most people who wear hats with sports logos are fans, or at least have some geographic and relational connection to the team. The problem is the statistical gap, and that is what makes for a stereotype. Though 95% of a group may fit a profile, it isn't 100%. By lumping in the remaining 5%, we are creating a stereotype and assuming a normality that does not exist. In addition, as discussed earlier, sometimes only 5% fit a profile, and we are the ones who add in the remaining 95%. If I asked you to describe the word *normal*, what would you say?

INABILITY TO DIFFERENTIATE

In a variety of professional settings and academic disciplines, we are taught about sympathy and empathy. There are different degrees of overlap between those two constructs, and application can be complicated. A simplified version is that sympathy reflects an awareness (and possible concern or compassion) that someone else is having a particular negative experience, such as pain. Empathy reflects a deeper level of recognition and awareness and may include a more profound understanding of the experience that someone else is having. In simple terms, sympathy may be described as "I recognize you are in pain." Empathy may be more "I feel (or have felt) your particular pain." As you might expect, there are varying degrees of both ideas.

We are encouraged to empathize with people, which is a good thing. The idea is to recognize and appreciate that people live different lives and that we should not be so egotistical that we consider our perspective or experience to be singular or superior. This is one of those ideas that people tend to agree with at face value, but we can still put our own life on a higher pedestal than others'. That elevation can be subtle and sometimes unconscious but still have a profound impact on decision-making. On a personal level, I do have some challenges with the construct. How in the world do I know what others are experiencing? Is the recognition of their experience just some level of sympathy? Can I get inside someone else's head and know how they process an event? The description and visual cues may be similar, but who is to say that our mindset also is aligned?

An example is our relative experiences of pain. If you have ever visited an urgent care facility or an emergency room, you may have been asked to rate your pain level on a scale of 1–10. This is an understandable question related to the triage of medical conditions. Essentially, the healthcare providers are trying to ascertain whether one person's pain is more urgent than that of the person sitting next to them in the waiting room. Undoubtedly, there are countless people who answer this question every day, but how do they determine what constitutes a 10, since pain can be such an individual experience? Some people are very sensitive to pain, while others can tolerate a great deal. The suggestion here is that, while we can be aware of other people's pain, we only truly understand our own. There is nothing wrong with this reality, but we must acknowledge that our barometer for evaluation is often filtered through our own, singular experience.

WORLDVIEW AND PACKAGE DEALS

People embody a variety of beliefs, and those collections are described with different words. *Religion. Philosophy. Ideology. Belief system. Perspective. Worldview.* That last word is important, because it is something all people have in their cognitive toolbox. Everyone has a worldview or, put another way, a view on the world. That worldview is based on a collection of cultural variables, upbringing, and ability or willingness to incorporate new ideas.

Our worldviews change over time as we learn, meet new people, and have new experiences. The changes may be major due to life-altering experiences, or they may be incremental as we age.

The ongoing question is whether we are aware of our own worldviews and the biases that ride along with our package of beliefs. As we age, certain beliefs may become more cemented as we are reluctant to question a construct that has shaped our reality for a very long time. Some people are more objective and can discern that some things in the world are worse than they were before, while others are better, and in some cases just different.

In the midst of a world that is always changing, we are constantly tasked with incorporating new ideas into our existing worldview. As you might expect, we do our best to create synergies of beliefs among the different facets of our belief system. For example, we may try to align our religion, politics, social views, parenting styles, and general behaviors as a citizen. This is a reasonable and rational practice, since living is hard enough without a bevy of inconsistencies in how we approach life, the universe, and everything in our experience.

Within the framework of our shifting worldview, we must struggle with assuming objectivity, ask for feedback, and evaluate whether there is true alignment. This is not a desirable cycle for many people who would rather stick with their beliefs through thick and thin and avoid the discomfort of ongoing evaluation. For Christ followers, a combination of factors can be employed. A rock-solid dedication to our belief that the Bible is the inspired Word of God is one thing. Believing that our favorite political beliefs are in alignment with Scripture just because we still stick with the party from our childhood is quite another.

Still, Christ followers must be careful. For example, earlier in the chapter I shared with you a bit of my background. I'm comfortable with that background and even maintain certain feelings of pride and loyalty to my hometown and various aspects of my upbringing. However, I strive to remember that this can still contribute to a myopic perspective. I grew up in a certain place, around certain people, was taught to think a certain way, and have maintained a certain lifestyle. These are all elements of my experience I constantly compared to those of other people, but familiarity does not make something right.

As I mentioned in chapter 4, the United States of America does a lot of things well. There is a long list of freedoms and opportunities. While I have not lived in another country, I have talked to people who have been around the world. As far as I can tell, I could live in worse places. That said, there is value in critiquing our homeland and wanting to always improve. There can be a razor-thin difference between pride in our country and arrogance.

For example, I have trouble with the song "God Bless America." The words are well-intended, but at times they can feel arrogant. Should we ask God to bless us at all, and is it even more presumptuous to ask for blessings for a singular country? It would not surprise me if my discomfort with this song were not appreciated by many people, and in particular American Christians. If I were to have a discussion with someone about this, I would likely ask whether my views are a challenge to their faith or to the link that has been established between faith and familiar civic activities. In other words, do we sing a song like this because its lyrics are familiar content that strengthens our sense of country? Or does it truly connect us to God?

ATTEMPTS TO BE OBJECTIVE

On a certain level, we are somewhat aware of our biases. We recognize and will sometimes admit our limited knowledge, as well as the reality that our perspective can be skewed by a variety of factors. That doesn't change the suggestion that our default position is often confidence in our own viewpoint. There are situations in which we attempt to guard against bias, and there are places in society where we talk about a so-called neutral third party, an observer, or a moderator. In many cases there are individuals and organizations that take their work seriously and do their best to limit editorial opinion. However, we always have a vested interest. It may not be particularly pressing or urgent, but there is always something. The very fact of being paid for our work means that we have an incentive built into the process.

In organizational life, leaders will often hire consultants. Why is that? What is the consultant going to tell them that they don't already know? Certainly, a consultant may be valuable in some situations and environments. There may be insights that an outsider can provide, or at least confirm. However, any consultant is going to want a positive review, and ultimately another gig. If the consultant tells the people what they should hear, as opposed to what they want to hear, will they get a recommendation for their next job? Perhaps. Are you more likely to listen to me if I admit my biases or if I say something that aligns with your existing beliefs?

I must give credit to a former student of mine, though his name escapes me, so I cannot properly cite my source. He said that humans tend to have what he called a base instinctual reaction. What he meant is that we can tend to have strong first reactions to people, places, and things we encounter. Our so-called instincts or impressions may be accurate or perceptive, but they can also be dead wrong. Once an impression is set, it can be hard to move away from our initial conclusion. Anecdote can quickly wipe away a huge amount of research, and the phrase "in my experience" or the idea of "my truth" can rule our biases. This is not to minimize what happens to real people, but as discussed above, it takes exactly one experience for a stereotype to be solidified.

THE GOOD SIDE—OR IS IT?

I grew up a fan of the *Star Wars* universe. I loved the movies, collected action figures, and replayed scenarios on the playground. When the first movie debuted in 1977, the characters and roles were established very quickly. Darth Vader and his Stormtroopers were the villains. Han Solo, Luke Skywalker, and Princess Leia were the primary heroes, along with their supporting cast of characters. This is a common literary mechanism, where we play a protagonist and an antagonist opposite each other in a narrative structure. We tend to like this setup because it keeps things simple. Who am I rooting for? That character? Great.

The problem is when we step back and look at the bigger picture. If we are honest, the Rebel Alliance is a terrorist organization. Certainly, Darth Vader is an angry character, and he seems to treat people very badly, so it is easy to root against him. However, his organization represents the establishment, and, at least according to their message, they want order and peace in the universe. Who could be against that? Then again, what if the so-called establishment is truly evil? What if the Rebels aren't terrorists but are in fact freedom fighters? Don't these determinations all depend on your upbringing, personal experience, and perspective?

Another example is perhaps more down-to-Earth (literally). A few years ago, a baseball team called the Houston Astros was punished by the league office for a cheating scandal involving stealing signs and using prohibited technology to gain an unfair advantage. I don't personally know many Astros fans, but I imagine this must have been frustrating. What do you do if you are a fan, particularly if you were born and raised to be a loyal supporter? Do you abandon the team for moral or ethical reasons? Or do you get defensive and talk about how other teams also cheat but never get caught? Overall, were fans of the Astros able to objectively evaluate the situation without the bias of loyalty?

As discussed earlier, some will argue that they are open-minded to new ideas. Abstractly, this may be true. We are presented with new ideas, products, processes, and perspectives every single day. When a new flavor of soda appears on the market, will I try it? Or will I conclude that the current soda is all I need and that I never, ever need to explore additional flavors? The answer is somewhere in the middle. Sometimes I embrace a new flavor. At other times I recognize that a new flavor may give other people satisfaction but that I don't need to try it.

If new ideas were restricted to soda flavors, we might have less conflict. Unfortunately, ideologies are often focused on more serious topics that challenge our core understanding of life. We must explore what open-mindedness means. So, I ask you, are you open-minded? Or are you open-minded to the things the world allows? Have you done some deep exploring of certain concepts, or are you simply a product of your environment? We like to think we have come up with our own thoughts, but change over time is subtle. What is deemed acceptable today may have been strictly forbidden in the past. Can we articulate why? Do we know the history of the attitudinal progression?

For example, we tend as a church to rank sins. There is certainly a hierarchy to be drawn from Scripture, particularly as it pertains to impact on large groups of people and on our unwillingness to repent. This is mirrored in our society when we quantify various crimes. However, on a theological level you could still argue that all manifestations of sin share a similarity in that all negative thoughts and actions represent disobedience to God. The caveat is that a study of church history suggests that we have not always focused on the same things. What is tolerated (or even embraced) today was perhaps forbidden in the past. Are we increasingly enlightened now? Or have our collective biases simply shifted?

Lest you think I am encouraging moral relativism to guard against bias, that is not my suggestion. Is there such a thing as being too open? Probably. At what point will you say *Enough*? The Christian artist Steve Taylor once sang, "You're so open-minded that your brain leaked out." I think he was alluding to the idea that open-mindedness is not a destination. There may be an openness to listening objectively but allowing absolutely anyone to do anything at any time is not being tolerant. That mindset is more indicative of a cognitive anarchy.

SELF-AWARE CHRIST FOLLOWERS

Sometimes our beliefs are not easy to articulate. Even if we admit that we are biased, we may struggle to explain our conclusions. People might say, "I don't know why I believe that . . . I just do." Others talk about a gut feeling, what is familiar or normal, or what their social circle believes. Sometimes people will admit that their beliefs, while not necessarily the right conclusion, are still hard to rationalize or explain away. Even if our brain tells us differently, such bias is hard to overcome. For example, I have a mild fear of heights. In some ways this fear is irrational. If I am on a high balcony, the likelihood of my body suddenly vaulting over the high railing that is ten feet away remains very low. Despite that, I still feel a little apprehensive when I walk out of those doors.

I have had many conversations with people, and sometimes I will ask for additional information. In other words, I ask them to back up their argument. Sometimes people can, but at other times they have no backing but still remain undeterred in their stance. They have a conviction, and they are going to stick with it no matter what. In some cases they quickly move to the suggestion that we "agree to disagree." There may be a justification for this conclusion in some cases, but there are situations when it feels as though people simply do not want to defend their biases.

In chapter 11 I will discuss technology and how it impacts our dialogue. At the risk of sounding crass, I'll quote a good friend of mine who once said, "Every dumbass has an encyclopedia in his pocket." The interesting element of that quote is that technology has given us instant access to vast amounts of information—but not necessarily knowledge or wisdom. Another way to look at this is that our smartphone provides limitless data that can be filtered to fit with our existing views. At the risk of including too many *Star Wars* references, an interesting line is spoken in *Star Wars: Episode II: Attack of the Clones*. A relatively minor character says to a supposedly trained and learned character, "I would think you Jedi would know the difference between knowledge and . . . wisdom."

There is another category of bias that is troubling, and it raises an interesting question. How honest do you want people to be? If we suspect that people are not being honest with us, we may complain that they are hiding their true feelings to avoid an argument or an awkward situation. However, when people are honest, there may be a complaint about the viewpoints that are being expressed. With that in mind, do we want people to be transparent, even if the ideologies they share are offensive to us and perhaps to large portions of the population?

This brings us to a final point, and that is our bias as Christ followers. I am unapologetically a Christ follower, and I will share that with anyone without shame. When I am with other Christ followers, it can be very affirming to be in community. We have shared beliefs and values, which creates commonality and a sense of spiritual family (chapter 1) that can be wonderful to experience. At the same time, this represents a bias on my part, and in many ways I embrace a narrow focus. While I seek to study, I don't intend to change the core of my worldview.

Despite my comfort with this personal bias, I know it might appear hypocritical to a reader who doesn't share my viewpoint. I've spent a whole chapter encouraging people to admit and confront their biases, but at the end I state that I love Jesus and that this isn't going to change. Am I going against the principles I have laid out? Yes and no. It is not necessarily wrong to have a biased perspective. The question is *which* bias. As discussed above, it is hard not to view the world through the lens of how we have been raised and influenced. The question is what we will do with this information. Will we continually seek to separate our worldly biases from scriptural teachings? Will we verbally admit that which we do not know, so that we can be open to learning new concepts? Only you can answer these questions, and we will explore them further in the next chapter.

PRACTICAL TIP

Ask someone you trust to list your biases for you. You might need to ask more than one person.

DISCUSSION QUESTIONS

1. Do you believe that you have certain biases or prejudices? Are you willing to share?
2. Can you point to what may have shaped your biases?
3. Do you embrace your biases, or do you work to overcome them?
4. Are there biases or prejudices that you consider to be a positive aspect of your personality and that you proudly defend?

6

CURIOSITY AND PARADIGM SHIFTS

HONESTY CHECK

How curious are you about new topics and ideas?

Let's start this chapter by talking about an important topic: socks. When I was young, I typically wore long, white tube socks. It was common to pull those socks up as high as they would go. This was the so-called normal, and most people adhered to the same fashion trend. Now that I am older, I often wear short, black socks. This is a seemingly insignificant shift in my behavior, but also interesting to analyze. Why is this the case? Was I slowly influenced by the powerful forces of the fashion industry, and am I simply a sheep? Should I have stood up to the nameless, faceless influences who took away my tube-sock freedom and replaced them with a new product of their design? Dramatic as this may sound, I'm happy with my socks. Or perhaps *they* have simply convinced me that I am happy. Regardless of why this occurred, it is interesting to think through changes of various kinds.

When I was in high school, I had a large stereo and some massive speakers. These speakers had wonderful sound quality, and I was sad when they finally started malfunctioning. Today's audio speakers are very good in terms of quality and tone, but they aren't the same as those old speakers. You can probably still acquire those speakers somewhere, but they aren't the norm. In some ways I miss them, and, perhaps more importantly, I feel as though I can articulate my attachment from a standpoint of frequency and fidelity. Granted, I must ask honest questions about this attachment, which is also not particularly significant in the grand scheme of life. Do I miss the actual speakers, or is there an element of nostalgia at play?

In the last chapter we talked about bias, and this is related to the topics of this chapter. Bias and paradigm shifts go hand in hand because they represent relative openness to new ideas. We must ponder not only whether we are capable of openness but whether we are willing to be open. There are some shifts that happen around us organically and may be harder to notice. Other changes are more overt, and we must decide whether we will fight trends or adapt to new mindsets. Part of this openness starts with a capacity for curiosity.

GRANDPA CURIOUS

My maternal grandfather is no longer living, but he lived into my late forties, so I had the privilege of knowing him from some of my earliest memories well into adulthood. On paper, my grandpa was not a highly educated man. He was born in a small town, did not progress in his education beyond the eighth grade, married a local girl, served in World War II, raised his family in a small town, and worked his whole life in a rural gas station and repair shop. My grandpa took a few trips, but I would not regard him as a particularly knowledgeable or well-read individual. His community was tight and supportive, but not particularly diverse in terms of lifestyle, demographics, or ideology. He worked hard, loved his family dearly, served his local church faithfully, and was one of those all-around good guys who was respected and appreciated in his local community. Despite his lack of education, one of the things I always appreciated about my grandpa was his consistent curiosity. He asked a lot of questions, and, while I got the sense that he didn't always understand the answers, he was genuinely intrigued by people, their professions, their travels, and their interests.

When I think about that mindset, I wonder whether that is one of those innate traits that just come naturally or whether curiosity can be fostered. Certainly, people can discipline themselves to ask questions out of politeness, but that doesn't mean that people are genuinely interested in new subjects. Part of parenting is teaching your children to ask certain questions of others so that they do not always focus on their own interests. However, can curiosity itself be taught? If I am honest, I must admit that I am simply uninterested in a variety of subjects. Some of this disinterest may stem from a recognition of how much time it would take to become marginally knowledgeable. For other subjects, I am simply not intrigued. This is the challenge for teachers everywhere. It is easy to learn and remember things when we are engaged. When we are bored, that is a much bigger challenge.

Behaviorally, there can be a frustrating gap between what we should do and what we feel led to do. I should probably be more interested in certain aspects of the world, but I am not.

One example is trees. My in-laws built a house, situated near a lake that was wooded. While some nearby neighbors cleared their land and installed large lawns, my in-laws wanted a more tree-filled area. They even planted more trees to create greater density. I remember walking through the yard and my wife asking, "What kind of tree is that?" I didn't know, and, truthfully, I didn't care. The trees were pretty, and I enjoyed them. I wasn't opposed to knowing, but researching the name of a given tree just didn't interest me.

OPEN TO WHAT IS NEW

Imagine you are at some sort of social gathering, such as a cocktail party. There are some people you know, but there are also individuals who are new to you, and inevitably you end up in a conversation with one of them. You exchange the usual pleasantries, which typically include name, what you do for a living, where you are from, and how you are connected to the host. Beyond that, how many additional questions do you ask? How deeply do you dig, and what happens if you don't make a connection with the person?

I can't make you curious, though I wish I had that power or a simple formula for its achievement. The truth is that I'm not always curious about everything, and sometimes that is bothersome. My brain tells me that curiosity or general interest is the right attitude for fostering dialogue with people, but that intrigue is sometimes difficult to manufacture. If I am honest, I don't always want to learn new things. People start talking about their interests, and, while I can discipline myself to keep my body language and face engaged, there are times when my mind has already left the building.

Likewise, I should always want to read new books, and, when given an opportunity to choose media, my brain tells me that I should watch thought-provoking documentaries and historical films that chronicle real-life events. The truth is that sometimes I want to watch a movie that is based on a comic book, and it is possible that I have seen it before. Or maybe seven times.

To be fair, there are many situations in which people are not necessarily closed-minded but still make choices that limit their need to try new things. My wife and I occasionally dine at a local pizza chain, and for a several-year stretch she ordered the same pizza every single time. She wasn't afraid of trying other menu items, but she enjoyed that pizza very much, and it represented a predictable quality. While there is value in this type of perspective, it has limits. It is one thing to find an acceptable solution to a problem. It is quite another to stubbornly refuse to *ever* consider other options.

THE TIMES, THEY ARE A-CHANGIN'

Times change. Trends change. When you look at the history of subjects like music, fashion, language, and human behavior, there are ample examples of how something popular eventually gives way to something else. Much as with other facets of life, some of this is good, some of this is bad, and some of it is just different. Are we able to understand impact, both in the short and in the long term?

When I was a child, one of the predominant methods for capturing pictures was with slides. People would take pictures of their vacation and then go home and get the slides developed by a professional who had specialized equipment. After that, consumers would take the slides, put them into a projector one by one, and project the images on the wall. The old slide projector would have a button that would advance the carousel to the next picture. As a child I have fond memories of family slide shows, where we would look at pictures of our past vacations or of things that had happened at different phases of our family's life.

There was one Christmas when we were all together and someone suggested getting out the old slide projector, even though the technology had advanced and this type of photographic capturing was no longer the standard way to store pictures. We got out the projector, loaded up some archived slides, and looked at some old pictures of when my parents were first married. In addition to enjoying some of the moments that had been captured, I can remember people laughingly critiquing the wardrobes. This is not an unusual instance, as dress-up days at school may include an attempt to replicate the fashions of the 1970s, 1980s, and other eras.

When people engage in these types of nostalgic activities, they often gravitate toward the most prominent stereotypes of that era. While these stylistic choices can make people laugh, they may forget that a given trend represented the height of fashion at one point. We may mock a prior era, but our own sense of so-called normality will eventually be noted by future generations. At this juncture some may again express a concern that this is a relativistic philosophy and that everything is justifiable and explainable under the broad umbrella of changing trends. There is some validity to this perspective, but it speaks to people's general attitude toward alterations in societal behavior. A key point is that our moment in time may appear somewhat "normal" but that normality is a moving target and something we should never take for granted.

INTRIGUED, ANNOYED, OR FEARFUL

Curiosity is not just about being intrigued by new ideas and wanting to expand your knowledge. It is also about allowing for the possibility that new things can be learned and that other solutions are possible. As mentioned in the last chapter, people tend to view the world through three different lenses. They may conclude that things are getting better, that they are getting worse, or that they may simply be different. To be fair, life is a combination of all three perspectives.

As discussed in the last chapter, humans can tend to have a base instinctual reaction to new ideas or concepts. During the COVID-19 pandemic, organizations were forced to roll out many new methodologies in order to maintain safety while also trying to survive as entities. One of those shifts was the use of QR codes on tables in restaurants so that fewer people had to touch menus. If you are not familiar with this technology, a QR code is a strange-looking graphic that a portable electronic device can scan with a digital camera. The graphic tells the camera to open an Internet site, which will display a particular type of information.

This is a minor example, but it creates a sort of mental test. These are not necessarily the only options, but consider this list of questions related to changes like the QR code menu. Do you find such changes to be:

1. An intriguing sign of positive development and innovation in society?
2. A troubling sign of negative societal shifts down a slippery slope?
3. A simple adjustment to the infrastructure of society that is mostly neutral and just something different?

Clearly, there are changes in society that can have elements of all three, but this may be difficult to analyze in the moment. In addition, as discussed in the last chapter, how much does bias play a role in how people evaluate adjustments to societal behaviors?

THE DREADED SLIPPERY SLOPE

Change evokes fear in many people, or at least a level of skepticism. To be fair, this is often a positive way to react. New information, ideas, and constructs should be evaluated carefully, and people should maintain a level of vigilance when it comes to incorporating changes. There should be a commitment to research and an attitude of patience. There are individuals who enjoy being so-called early adopters of innovation, but these decisions should still be approached with care.

The challenge is that some individuals struggle with a general attitude of apprehension toward anything that is different from their perception of the norm. As Christ followers, we maintain an understanding that we live in a sinful world and that all we do has the potential to fall into darkness. At the same time, we understand the redeeming power of God's grace and that His goodness is on display through the wonders of creation. In other words, positive change can occur in society. God has entrusted us with gifts of innovation and creativity, which can be applied to positive impacts in our world.

This perspective is not shared by everyone. For some people, new perspectives are not seen as positive change but as attempts at indoctrination. Choices to abandon past practices may solicit skepticism, and people worry that decision-makers are being impacted by negative forces in a sinful world, such as pressure from financiers or the influence of political agendas that skew toward depraved thinking.

Over the years many educational institutions have changed their mascots. Some of these mascots represented symbols that are no longer viewed as appropriate. Examples include various people groups that are portrayed simply as bloodthirsty warriors or mascots that are associated with historical events that represent a troubling association. For some alumni of these institutions, changing mascots has been viewed negatively; they see these changes as the result of misguided reactions to an overly sensitive society. The counter to this argument is that some of these issues do not put society on a path toward moral destruction. Perhaps the mascot should stay the same. Or perhaps that mascot was innocently intentioned but should never have been selected in the first place.

THE ENERGY TO PURSUE

People will work hard in a variety of arenas. Individuals get up every day, put in a lot of hours in the marketplace and at home, and are often required to acquire new skills and learn additional information. Other times people just don't want to put in the effort. In general, this is an understandable approach to life. If we can avoid dedicating additional physical or mental energy to a task, there may be wisdom in conserving our resources. On balance, the question is whether we are being efficient or being stubborn or close-minded.

Every person must answer a simple question on a regular basis. How much energy do I want to put toward learning new things beyond what is immediately required of me to maintain something like a professional job? Will I seek out new perspectives simply because they may enhance my knowledge? Do I allow for the possibility that new ideas will not only give me additional data points but might also shift the way in which I see the world in general? Does that excite me or frighten me?

The energy to pursue change (or to begrudgingly accept it) can become harder to come by for people as they get older. Over time I have helped older people with technology, which often encompasses computers, mobile phones, or Internet navigation. These people are not unintelligent. In fact, some of them are or have been accomplished thinkers. They have raised families, worked hard at jobs, lived through decades of change, and overcome a host of obstacles. However, for some reason the parts of their brain that can acquire certain new information have worn down. Something doesn't quite compute (no pun intended). What is easy for a younger person can be painstaking for an older individual. This doesn't make them a bad person, but it can be frustrating when the learning is slow or does not seem to occur at all.

Sometimes people simply do not feel like thinking, and that includes me. This is not just a difficulty for old people who are struggling to work their new device. The lack of energy to explore new ideas starts at birth and continues until death. Part of the process of dialogue is to encourage people to consider new ideas rather than to simply place existing viewpoints opposite one another.

PARADIGM SHIFTS AND PERSPECTIVES

A paradigm is defined by one source as "a philosophical or theoretical framework of any kind." In simpler terms, a paradigm is a structure by which people organize anything into standardized and predictable patterns. This concept is used in a variety of industries, and it helps people establish a way to predict future variables. Using tables or methods of prediction can be very helpful and efficient, but use of a paradigm can also cause people to ignore other possibilities because different ideas do not fit the established pattern.

There is also a construct called a paradigm shift. One definition is "a fundamental change in approach or underlying assumptions." This concept refers to the idea that sometimes an entire system needs to be reevaluated. The original construction of the system may have been pursued with good intent. However, certain interpretations of variables led to a paradigm that was flawed from the beginning, or at least failed to take into account some missing content.

When we discuss a paradigm shift, what we are talking about goes beyond adjustments. Buying a new flavor of creamer you find at a store represents a small example of your willingness to try something new and accept a minor risk. A more fundamental shift is deciding to give up drinking coffee altogether after having enjoyed two to three cups per day for thirty years.

In a church setting, paradigm shifts may occur when new pastors are hired or leadership decides to change the core programs of a long-standing congregation. For some, a paradigm shift is an opportunity for a welcome change. For others it represents an unwelcome alteration to their way of processing normalcy. When this occurs, there can be immediate tension.

Related to the idea of paradigm shifts is the concept of divergent thinking. The framework of divergent thinking is related to what we would label as creativity. Divergent thinking is not just about unique ideas but also suggests that there may be multiple solutions to a need or problem. Pursuing divergent thinking is about seeking to get outside standardized methods and allow for nonlinear, free-flowing analysis that maximizes possible options. Can a workforce that sat at desks for years adapt to an office setting that mixes stand-up desks, common work areas, and various remote locations? Will a culture that is used to eating fish, chicken, pork, and beef be willing to convert to a system of eating where the primary protein comes from insects? These are just a couple of examples, but they speak to whether people groups are truly willing to think differently about how the world works.

WHAT IS YOUR PARADIGM?

Earlier in the book I discussed the variable of culture, and in the prior chapter I talked about the construct of bias. When you visit another country, you realize very quickly that your home country is your paradigm for normalcy in terms of language and cultural practices. There is a difference between studying a language and being immersed in a culture to a point that you start to understand that certain words don't translate cleanly from one language to another. People not only speak differently but also think differently.

Whether people realize their inability to adjust is a complicated question. There have certainly been times when people have struggled to adjust, even for seemingly inconsequential items. In 1992 the Pepsi company debuted a product called Crystal Pepsi. The carbonated beverage was engineered to have the established taste of Pepsi but with one fundamental difference. This product was clear instead of the traditional brown color that has been historically associated with cola flavors.

After much hype and initial interest, the company pulled the product from the shelves two years after its release. Among other reasons, the public could not force a paradigm shift involving flavor and appearance. Even when something is carefully explained, there comes a point at which people are unable (or unwilling) to alter their mindset. This is an ongoing key challenge of dialogue, and something that will be discussed in the rest of the book.

When it comes to mental paradigm shifts, can the ability to think differently be learned? Or are some people simply born or raised with a cognitive rigidity that inhibits their ability to comprehend different thought processes? These are difficult questions, and issues that scientists, theologians, and various other thinkers continue to debate.

A PATHWAY TO DIALOGUE

During the COVID-19 pandemic, some congregations switched to online services. This was lamented by many congregants who missed the opportunity to gather. There were also some who wondered aloud whether church leaders should comply with government regulations. Switching to virtual worship or canceling altogether was frustrating for many, but it did provide a chance to evaluate the common practice of corporate gatherings. What was missed? Was it certain content that is better translated in person? Or seeing friends and familiar faces? Perhaps it was simply being out and about?

The key purpose of this chapter is to highlight the importance of openness to new ideas. A caveat to this perspective is that there is also wisdom in skepticism and vigilance, as not all new ways of thinking are healthy or beneficial. An openness to a variety of approaches is not just about enhancing knowledge but also about recognizing our own limits and understanding. The usual concerns about slippery slopes can certainly be observed, but introspection should be an ongoing process for people.

Admittedly, deep thought and objective evaluation may not come naturally. Exploring, research, and journeys of discovery take time and effort, which are often in short supply. In addition, our simply being open to new ideas does not mean that they will be understood and absorbed into our ideology. Paradigm shifts do not always happen cleanly, and there can be long periods of mental tension.

There is an older man in my church who routinely invites different people to breakfast. His goal is to get to know people better and to keep learning. I have had breakfast with this individual a couple of times, and it is an encouraging experience. He asks a lot of questions, and he pays attention to his surroundings. In some ways he can still be a grumpy senior citizen who is comfortable with his way of life, but his approach to new ideas gives me hope.

One other issue to note is that a paradigm shift may point Christ followers or the church in a more biblical direction. What if the way we have been doing things all along has been an inferior or less than effective way? What if our church practices, though well-intentioned, have been more about familiar historical rituals than Scripture? Also, it is important to keep in mind that dedicating your life to Christ is itself a definite paradigm shift. In 2 Corinthians 5:17 Paul points out, "Therefore, if anyone is in Christ, the new creation has come: The old has gone, the new is here!" Is there anything old that needs to pass away in your life?

PRACTICAL TIP

If you have ever thought or verbalized that someday you want to learn something about a new topic, today is the day. Not someday. Someday may never come.

DISCUSSION QUESTIONS

1. Would you describe yourself as a curious person? How do you know? Has your curiosity changed over time?
2. Is the world better than, worse than, or just different from what it was before?
3. If you are honest, do you like change?
4. Can you identify paradigm shifts you have experienced in your life?

7

EMOTIONS, DISTRACTIONS, AND LISTENING

HONESTY CHECK

When you have a conversation with someone, how much of the time do you talk and how much do you listen? If the topic is more serious or controversial, are you prone to any emotions, and to what degree does that impact your focus on mutual understanding?

Are you feeling emotional right now? How do you know this to be true? Are you able to draw clear distinctions between so-called thoughts and feelings? Can you turn feelings on and off like a light switch or control them with ease? Do any of these questions I am asking cause your blood pressure to rise? What we have come to deem as emotions are a complicated combination of physiological experiences, behaviors, and reactions to situations. One dictionary defines emotion as "a natural instinctive state of mind deriving from one's circumstances, mood, or relationships with others." Another definition suggests that emotion is "instinctive or intuitive feeling, as distinguished from reasoning or knowledge."

When we consider the biological, psychological, and cultural aspects of what we label as emotion, it is hard to come up with a clean definition. With apologies to Supreme Court Justice Potter Stevens, we may struggle to define emotion, but we know it when we see it.

In some ways, emotion is a beautiful aspect of our humanity. Emotion can sometimes be the fuel for positive feelings that include versions of love, joy, and pleasure. The challenge is that emotion is also linked to anger, fear, and sadness. These are not feelings we enjoy. In addition, those so-called feelings can ebb and flow and can be difficult to sustain when paired with a connection to people or a cause. For some, emotion can express itself as a roller-coaster of feelings that rise and fall by the minute and are difficult to control. When it comes to productive dialogue, emotions can infuse energy into conversation, but they can also be a definitive distraction. In this chapter we will discuss the role emotions play in conversation, and how we deal with focus and effective listening.

HOW DO WE MEASURE?

The phrase in the dictionary about emotion being "distinguished from reasoning or knowledge" is interesting, and perhaps a little troubling. When I asked you whether you are emotional right now, that was a serious question but also a minor test of your definition. If I also asked you at any given moment whether you were reasonable or knowledgeable, what might you say? There are cognitive tests that attempt to measure emotion, but most of our assessment is based on subjective observation of shifting behaviors. In addition, there is the question of whether we ourselves are the best judge of our own feelings and how they impact the world around us.

Can you be devoid of emotion in every situation, or are our emotions always present in some form? Can you experience a calm, measured rage that isn't visually obvious? Might you simply have active tear ducts that regularly produce liquid and make you appear sensitive? Is it possible that some of your active and present emotions do not include obvious, visible signs, while others are hard to hide? It is difficult to suggest that we are never without some form or level of emotion. Every moment of every day has aspects of joy, sadness, pleasure, fear, and anxiety. The levels obviously change depending on the person or situation, but a total absence of emotion is harder to defend.

A commonly used evaluation is the Myers-Briggs assessment, the results of which include a choice of four pairs of single-letter variables. The person who has taken this test may tell you that they have been categorized as an ENTJ, an ISFP, or an ESFJ. Without explaining the whole test, one pairing is T/F, which stands for "Thinking" and "Emotion." A test-taker is assigned either a T or an F, depending on their responses. The premise of this pairing is that test-takers are more prone to making decisions via so-called rational thought versus emotion. This obviously depends on a combination of answers, and the test may also reveal a range that indicates whether a person is a stronger or weaker T or F.

When people take these types of tests, the results may serve as confirmation of what they had already suspected to be true. However, many researchers will caution the universal application of self-evaluations. Humans, it would seem, cannot be universally trusted to answer truthfully or with total self-awareness. As discussed, there is also the challenge of meaning. Is it easy for us to differentiate the decision-making process for a strong thinker versus a feeler? Is the person who scores high on emotion unable to form rational thoughts? That is a hard argument to make. Is the high-scoring thinker a machine that cannot feel anything beyond their almost robotic pathways for making cold, lifeless decisions? This also is a problematic conclusion. What we must grasp is that rationality and emotion are often subjective and intertwined and may always walk together even if the combination can tie up a person in knots.

EMOTIONS IN CONVERSATION

When it comes to conversation, it is fair to suggest that we can feel strongly about certain issues. Notice that word choice: *feel*. Not reason, and not think. We use what we have come to label as an emotion-based word to describe the depth of our convictions. The presence of strong feelings may motivate us, but they can also distract us, which makes listening to others all the harder. Listening is especially difficult if we can neither articulate our reactions nor set them aside. Some understand that they are particularly vested in or passionate about issues and that their strong feelings may cloud their judgment. Others struggle to admit that reality.

Earlier in the book I talked about the construct of passion, which can have both positive and negative applications, depending on the context. If someone appears to be calm and articulate, could they still be a raging inferno of passion on the inside? Sure. Is there value in raising your voice to show that you really care about something? Uh, maybe? What is the difference between passionate and being obsessed? Hmmm . . . that is tougher. As with emotion, measuring passion can be difficult and subjective, and the intensity can waver in the moment.

When it comes to our personal emotions and how they impact dialogue, it can be difficult to maintain a balance between anecdote and data-driven conclusions. An objective, researched approach to an issue may be more informed and comprehensive, but external sources can easily be set aside due to personal experience. A mountain of research studies may be irrelevant to the person for whom a profound event has shaped their understanding of a subject. Again, this can be both positive and negative.

From time to time I donate platelets, which is a more specialized form of giving blood. This process takes much longer in terms of time and can be very tiring on a physical level. I started donating because of a direct connection to people going through a difficult treatment for a rare disease. Helping other humans is a good practice in general, but for me this act is very personal. The treatment path for my friends ended many years ago, but I continue to donate, and I am fueled by a combination of altruism and grief.

If someone were to ask whether I have an emotional connection to donating platelets, I would readily and unapologetically admit to this reality. Furthermore, if I were to be asked whether other human needs are less important to me because there isn't a personal connection, I might just have to admit that as well. This is where our ties to people and ideas can get tricky. Can we acknowledge that something or someone is important to us but does not need to have the same value in our minds as it might to someone else? Or do we expect our perspective to be adopted by everyone? When it comes to concepts in general, are we able to admit to our seemingly irrational "gut" feelings?

Due to elements of subjectivity, we must recognize that emotion can look different to various people. In addition, pointing out the presence of emotion can create division quickly.

For example, telling someone that they are emotional and not rational does not typically go well. Do we really want emotion to be removed, though, from decision-making? Even if we did, would we know how to make a clean separation? It is difficult to neatly wrap up the complex construct of emotions, but we must be vigilant in terms of how they impact our individual decisions, along with our dialogue with others.

PARTY CONVERSATIONS

In addition to emotions, we can struggle to focus due to a variety of distractions. Emotions are one challenge, and the world around us can provide plenty of external noise. Despite our best attempts, we can struggle to multitask and handle more than one channel of content at a time. Many of you have been in a party or other social situation that involves crowds of people and many conversations in pairs or small groups. Throughout the gathering you may go from conversation to conversation and sometimes physically move around a room. At one point you might start a conversation with an individual or small group, but partway through that conversation you take notice of a separate conversation that is happening within earshot of your own dialogue.

For one or more reasons, that other conversation turns out to be more interesting than the one in which you are currently participating. Because the person you are talking to is still speaking (sometimes without an obvious end point) and you are a generally polite individual, you feel compelled to appear interested and attentive. In truth, you are trying to listen to the other conversation while at the same time listening just enough to your current interaction that you wouldn't get embarrassed if the person were to ask you a question. This can be a mentally frustrating, and even exhausting task, not to mention extremely difficult.

Keep in mind that this is just one example because distractions come in many forms. When we are in a group setting or one-on-one, we can struggle to focus. Our mind gets bored, we see movement that draws us away, or our physical energy level drops to the point that we have difficulty maintaining our attention on what is in front of us. If you have watched various creatures in the animal kingdom, you know that some are constantly in motion. Some of this is a defense mechanism against predators, but when you watch birds or squirrels in the park, it seems that they are almost designed to be distracted by every little thing. We may believe that we are more sophisticated and in control of our thoughts and actions, but sometimes we are no less likely to flit from one thought or stimulus to another. The world is filled with shiny objects, and sometimes we are the squirrel, running around and trying to find the most interesting item to chew on.

STATIC

I don't know how some technology works, but I do know that there are various devices, wires, and transmitters that send text, music, pictures, and video around the world in a flash. We have developed some incredible advancements in technology, but I don't truly understand how content on my device can miraculously get to another device around the world in a matter of seconds. It is particularly interesting to ponder the wireless world, where information seemingly travels through the air and somehow doesn't get lost along the way. Somehow it all seems to work most of the time.

To be fair, it doesn't always work. Technology is always a work in progress. Files get lost. Calls get dropped. Texts and emails don't go through. Even with our rapidly advancing technology, a driver will still hear pronounced static when they drive far enough from a radio tower or enter a tunnel. The same thing happens when we dialogue, but, in the case of humans, there may be more interference than we realize. Instead of static, there may be times when someone sends over a mental picture and we are able only to translate a random collection of pixels.

In the field of organizational behavior, theorists have studied what happens when a person attempts to communicate information to a listening party. That information can be presented in various forms, but once it is transmitted there is still a process of receiving, decoding, organizing, and analyzing. Again, the transmission process can be interrupted by distraction and noise from a variety of sources. The information that arrives may be tainted by previously discussed bias or fail to be fully understood due to lack of knowledge. In other words, some dialogue is invariably lost in translation. Can this be mitigated? It can, to a point.

PLEASE PAY ATTENTION

In the field of communication, theorists have established a construct called active listening. The definition and structure of this idea vary, but it often centers on encouraging listeners to focus on presented content, and in some cases repeat it back to the speaker. For example, the listener might say, "What I heard you say is . . ." This signals to the speaker that the listener is not only attuned to what is being said but can succinctly summarize the content. It may seem like too much effort to repeat everything, but sometimes this is a necessarily process to encourage disciplined focus.

It is reasonable to suggest that this process can be developed through practice and coaching, but there is still a fundamental challenge. Do we have to decide to listen? As with curiosity in the last chapter, we sometimes label particular people as good listeners. The term is almost an acknowledgment that others don't tend to listen as well, but this does not tell us whether shortcomings are the result of undeveloped skill or simple lack of motivation. In other words, are some people just not interested in listening to others?

Every chapter starts with an Honesty Check, so consider this a special, mid-chapter bonus quiz. When you think about conversations you have on a regular basis, are there times when you simply do not care about what others are saying? Remember, be honest. Again, this was discussed in the last chapter when I talked about curiosity. Even if you are disciplined enough to sit in front of a person and listen to them talk, are you unable to manufacture any level of intrigue?

To be fair, some people don't know what to ask. They may understand that they should be curious but may struggle to come up with relevant questions. There are also individuals who struggle with narcissism to the point that they will literally talk about themselves throughout an entire conversation. I've had conversations with people in which I ask them all sorts of biographical questions without them asking a single question in return. We often see this type of behavior in children, and friendly adults will indulge kids in this area because the little ones don't know any better. Their world is much smaller and understandably self-focused. As people age, we expect them to grow in their understanding that there is more to life than just their interests. Unfortunately, this realization does not always develop, even in seemingly mature adults.

MULTITASKING AND MOTIVATION

As much as we think that we can multitask, this is a constant struggle for the average human. Yes, we can sometimes walk and chew gum at the same time, but there is a reason some people have gotten lost in conversation and then walked right into a pole. Our brain can simply have a hard time processing too many pieces of information. We are constantly distracted by sound, movement, and other thoughts (and emotions) that enter our minds. Therefore, we can have a hard time memorizing various types of information. At some point our brain is "full." Or tired. Or bored. Or distracted. Or simply disengaged. I'm sorry, what were we talking about?

Our struggles with multitasking can impact our ability to listen. Have you ever been in a situation in which you were conversing with another person and they said something back to you that implied they weren't listening to what you had just said? This is not an uncommon occurrence. Perhaps they are paying attention in a general sense. However, if I speak for a couple of minutes and verbalize five different pieces of information while someone else is letting me talk, the listener may key in on one thing I said and start mentally preparing a response. For this example, let's call it Item #2. When they do respond, their rebuttal may already be outdated and irrelevant because I covered what they were thinking in my Item #4. Unfortunately, part of the listener's brain stopped processing new information because they were fine-tuning their response while patiently (or perhaps impatiently) waiting for me to stop speaking.

This again brings up the question of motivation. Do people want to listen, or are they just pausing politely before they make their next point? A good test is often body language and the propensity of the listener to respond with haste. In some cases, listeners (or maybe we should just call them responders) will interrupt the speaker before they are finished because they can't wait to share their perspective. This type of back-and-forth dialogue is not always negative, but it can signal an unwillingness on the part of one or both parties to fully consider content before answering.

I'M SORRY, WHAT WAS THE QUESTION?

To be honest, I don't know whether the game of telephone is played any longer. When I was growing up this game was occasionally played at school or church events, oftentimes as a so-called icebreaker. The game was reasonably straightforward. A group of people sat in a circle, and the game was typically more entertaining if the group was large. The first person whispered a phrase into the ear of the second. That person was tasked with whispering it into the ear of the third person, and so on. A key rule was that the phrase could not be repeated, so if the listener did not quite understand they could not ask for clarification. What you heard (or thought you heard) was what you passed on. This was part of the entertainment, as it was often obvious via facial expression that a person did not quite understand what had been whispered in their ear. Once the phrase reached the last person, they would state it aloud, and the first person would either confirm or clarify. Depending on the ability of people to whisper, hear, and overcome ambient noise in the room, what was eventually passed via human "telephone" might have become lost in translation along the way.

A functional difficulty of listening and dialogue involves staying on topic. In a friendly conversation, it may be natural and acceptable to cover a variety of subjects. The phrase "that reminds me" may serve as a transition between topics, which can lead to what people have come to label as a flight of ideas. In his book *Brain Rules: 12 Principles for Surviving and Thriving at Work, Home, and School*, author and researcher John Medina suggests that many studies point to humans having short attention spans, along with an inability to focus on one topic. In fact, he suggests that some people can only focus for less than ten minutes before they need their brain to be jostled. That is bad news for pastors who preach long sermons or professors who deliver long lectures. When it comes to topical focus in basic conversation, that time may be even shorter depending on the person and subject matter.

Another challenge we must recognize is that dialogue and debate can sometimes get confused. There are those who are cleverer with how they present certain arguments, which has given rise to debate clubs at high schools across the world. In addition, there are many situations in which people do not understand the content that is being discussed. Rather than asking for clarification, they change the subject before it becomes more obvious that they are lost. This phenomenon happens in a variety of facets throughout our everyday lives.

When people conduct research, there is a concerted effort to separate variables. This is a statistical challenge that plagues all researchers and something many people do not fully understand. Correlation is not causation, but it is easy for an unaware individual or population to conclude that two variables are causally linked. When that occurs, that individual will struggle to accept alternatives. They may politely listen to someone explain other ideas, but their mind may be fixated on their schema, which distracts them from having a more open-minded approach.

SOME THOUGHTS ON LISTENING

Much of this chapter focuses on the challenges of daily interactions and the psychology that can plague our dialogue. Ultimately, we must ask a few self-reflection questions. When you encounter an opinion or person you disagree with, how much of your brain says "Maybe I have the wrong approach"? Do we sabotage our own ability to listen and equally compare their beliefs to our prior viewpoints? Do we approach conversations with the attitude of "Maybe I will learn something new"? Or do we ask ourselves whether we have an attitude that says "I *want* to learn something new"? Do we think we are able to learn new things? Do we fear learning? Do we want to be challenged? Depending on how we answer all these questions, how does this impact our ability or willingness to listen?

In the end (and the beginning), we must step outside our earthly knowledge and continually consult Scripture. The gifts God has given us can help us discern, which is why we should continually study behavior, seek to understand research, and utilize a variety of cognitive tools. Scripturally, when it comes to emotions, distractions, and listening, there is always value in consulting the book of James. I love this book because James just says it like it is.

James 1:19–21 says, "My dear brothers and sisters, take note of this: Everyone should be quick to listen, slow to speak and slow to become angry, because human anger does not produce the righteousness that God desires. Therefore, get rid of all moral filth and the evil that is so prevalent and humbly accept the word planted in you, which can save you." These are very direct verses, and James experientially knew the heart of the sinner. We may seek to do good, but we know that our intent is selfish. Even a secular world has some sense of this. The world may not understand sin, but many recognize that humans are prone to a Machiavellian (scheming, cunning, and unscrupulous) intent.

Despite our best intentions, we often approach dialogue with some simple question. Namely, What is in it for me? or How can I benefit from this situation? In addition, we must continually ask broader questions, which are impacted by sinful emotions and the distractions of a secular society. Are we truly altruistic? Can we admit to our sinful nature? Again, there are wonderful people in this world who truly love their human brothers and sisters. However, on some level our dialogue will always be self-serving. In the next chapter we will discuss how this self-serving attitude can translate to our attitudes toward like-minding thinkers.

PRACTICAL TIP

Make a list of emotions that you consider to be regularly present in your life and write a sentence by each one that describes the roles it plays in your decision-making.

DISCUSSION QUESTIONS

1. What comes to mind when you think about emotion? What role should emotions play in your day-to-day life and decision-making?
2. Are you a "good" listener, and would people who know you agree with your self-assessment?
3. If you are honest, are you interested in other people's opinions? Do you tend to get distracted?
4. Do you think good listening skills can be learned? What role should emotions play in conflict resolution?

8

COMMUNITIES AND ECHO CHAMBERS

HONESTY CHECK

Are you interested in meeting new people, or are you content with your current circle of friends and family? Do different cultures, communities, and cultures intrigue you, or do you find them to be strange or even conclude that their approaches and behaviors are wrong?

There is a pragmatism to commonality. After all, why spend your limited time on this planet with people you don't like very much? That may be a somewhat selfish way to frame our existence, but an honest appraisal of humanity suggests that people stick with known paradigms. There are exceptions, as some people are energized by new individuals, ideas, and perspectives. Seeking diversity can richly enhance the human experience, but on a general level it is still reasonably common to hang out with like-minded people. Overall, this is not necessarily a negative aspect of the human experience. When it comes to the church, its whole purpose is to be unified in our pursuit of being like Christ. A congregation that is focused on kingdom work is an exciting reality.

With regard to your own community, have you ever done an audit of your social circle? Whom do you hang out with on a regular basis? If an outsider were to evaluate your close friends, how would they describe them? To be fair, our individual community is often a result of our environment. We don't always get to choose the people on our college dorm floor or our co-workers in our department. When we move into an apartment or house, we don't get to select our neighbors. However, to a certain extent we make choices that impact where we live, work, and hang out. We make choices when it comes to social events, dating, church, and community engagement. Those choices are a combination of conscious and unconscious decisions, and they often reveal a deeper reality in identifying our bias toward our chosen community.

THE GOOD STUFF OF BEING TOGETHER

Let us start out on an uplifting note. *Community* is often a positive word, and it can be an indication that humans are living in happy harmony. The word *community* can mean many things, including a defined geographic area where people live or a group that shares similar interests, goals, or ideology. It is fair to suggest that human beings tend to be happier when they are part of an affirming and stable community. Even if we maintain a sense of individuality, it is not uncommon for us to define ourselves by our community. We self-identify as a member of a larger group. While we may not state this idea specifically, a community gives us a positive sense that at least one collective out there has accepted us into their membership. We belong somewhere, even if that sphere is small.

There are myriad ways to dissect and define different communities around the world, and that goes beyond the scope of this book. What is apparent is that people spend a great deal of energy pursuing, developing, and maintaining communities. Some communities happen by design, others are spontaneous, and some develop as the result of an unforeseen event. Regardless of origin, communities are a big deal in human society. People will move entire families to engage with a desirable community or escape one that is no longer acceptable to them. It is not uncommon for people to pay dues, attend meetings, and follow certain rules just so they can be part of a certain organization.

Community is also part of our legacy. As Christians we should not focus on our earthly impact, but we still like the idea that our group will live on. Therefore, people give money to campaigns for new buildings on a college campus (with their names associated with these projects). There are times when nostalgia causes us to romanticize our association with certain communities, but this can also be a positive manifestation of our ongoing values. If a group or organization continues to embody the identity that has become familiar to us, and this has been sustained over time, it can give us a strong sense of satisfaction to identify with something bigger than ourselves.

HOW DO YOU DEFINE YOURSELF?

We often define ourselves by our respective communities. As we discussed in chapter 1, that starts with family, which is another reason familial strife is so painful. That is our base community, so when it goes awry we can be deeply discouraged over losing our biological community. Our membership also includes our workplace; geography; the sports teams we support; and our chosen religion, church, or denomination. We define ourselves by gender, sexuality, race, ethnicity, and lifestyle. This is another reason discrimination can be such a challenge in society. When people discriminate, they aren't just limiting the person; they are directly or symbolically taking on an entire community group.

Some of our communities are more superfluous, and in certain cases almost playful. Still, there is the subtle reality that they form at least part of our identity. I was once the editor for a sports blog called Emerald City Swagger. As of the writing of this book, I am the bass player for a small, community-based band called Children of Disorder. Do these random factoids define me? To a certain extent, yes. They represent small communities of which I am a part. However, it would be inaccurate to suggest that these minor alliances represent my core values, identity, and worldview.

Sports can be a great unifier of people, particularly in geographic areas. When people wear hats, jerseys, and other fan gear, this can make a connection between total strangers who see each other in public and acknowledge their shared allegiance to the football team. This can be particularly true when two fans encounter each outside their home turf. It is as though two missionaries have found solace as they navigate being pilgrims in an unholy land. In some cities there are identified bars where out-of-town fans will gather to watch their favorite team. There may be nothing else that connects this group of people, but they are still drawn to a common experience.

Some communities aren't quantifiably definable groups of people with a formal association or organized membership. For example, sometimes we define ourselves by where we have been, what we have accomplished, or what unique experiences have occurred in our life. People who have climbed Mount Everest are in an elite class of climbers. Likewise, individuals who have visited the South Pole represent a small segment of the global population. People in these groups may not know each other, but they can claim a membership that is not shared by many others.

Some of these associations are simply factual and do not play an active role in day-to-day life. There are certain groups that people regularly embrace, while others are just there and may never come up in conversation. The key question that remains is often about membership and identity and how people express that status to the rest of the world. This leads us to questions of openness and whether there is an obvious sense of welcoming—or perhaps a bouncer at the door.

THE CHALLENGES OF CLOSED DOORS

The word *pride* is complicated. There are many situations in which pride can be a positive aspect of life and community. People take pride in their work, family, and heritage. Parents feel a positive sense of pride when their children achieve worthy goals. Professionals can be proud to work for an organization that has a meaningful impact on the world. Positive vibes of pride can flow when communities rally around a cause or need by displaying selflessness and generosity.

Of course, pride can also be a definitively negative part of human behavior. A sense of pride can quickly lead to feelings of elitism and superiority. This can cause people and groups to look down on others and create a hierarchy of social importance. Some groups express their pride in isolation, while others look to demonstrate power over other communities. Unfortunately, this has caused devastating violence throughout human history, ranging from petty verbal squabbles to heartbreaking episodes of genocide.

How hard is it to break into your community? Is there an application, a fee, or an interview? Are there certain people who will never qualify? Or are there subtle indications that people are not necessarily welcome to apply or join? Some doors are the result of economic realities. While we don't have the time to unpack the complexities of economics and equal access to basic human needs, there is at least some acceptance or understanding in society that not everyone can have the so-called (earthly) nice things. That said, this is a much more nuanced question than who can afford to purchase big-ticket items.

Evaluating access is about measuring whether a wide spectrum of individuals is not just allowed but feels openly welcomed to join a particular community. For Christ followers, this starts and ends with the church. A warm handshake and the physically open doors of a church sanctuary are one part of this discussion, but the construct of openness encompasses a much bigger picture.

THE CHALLENGE OF CLOSED MINDS

In a literal sense, an echo chamber is a purposely designed physical space that creates reverberation. This space is often used to create intentional types of acoustic settings, such as a music studio. This type of room can be very useful for certain purposes, but there is one key factor. The sound does not typically get out, and, more importantly, sound from outside does not get in. An "echo chamber" is also a phrase that is used in a symbolic sense to describe a situation in which beliefs are reinforced within the confines of a closed system. The enclosure is not literal, but it still functions as a cognitive room where new ideas neither get in nor out.

Admittedly, the belief-oriented echo chamber is a conceptual idea. Much as people have a so-called invisible bubble around them that functions as a comfort zone in different environments, so also there is a mental barrier that people will not cross from an ideological standpoint. Instead of seeking out new ways of thinking, the echo chamber bounces existing beliefs back to the individual or group, typically with a dose of affirmation. I will discuss some of the impacts of technology later, but we have seen this in social media with platforms that allow others to express support for an idea through simple responses such as a comment, smiley face, or thumbs-up. Support can obviously be a good thing, but it can also limit discussion and give the original person the idea that theirs is the only way of thinking.

We all live in some version of a closed community that could be described as an echo chamber—or, more accurately, many echo chambers. We live in a society that seeks affirmation. Did I get the right answer? Are my facts straight? Did I follow the instructions correctly? Is this the right tool to use? Much of this positive feedback can be a good thing. We want the surgeon to be accurate. We want to grab the right sized socket for our wrench. However, what about thinking and more conceptual ideas? Are we satisfied with asking for fixed answers from groups of people who may or may not be experts in certain fields? What if there is a better way of thinking?

The phrase "If it ain't broke, don't fix it" may be a solid response to certain functional areas of life. Unfortunately, it can be a concerning sign that individuals or groups have consciously chosen to limit or exclude new ways of thinking. There is a reasonable amount of vigilance that should be applied to different ways of thinking, as various philosophies can lead people astray. However, familiarity should never be seen as a guarantee of right thinking. What if something were designed adequately but poorly in the first place, and a group simply accepted the solution because they did not know that there was potentially a better way?

Ultimately, there is a fine line between group focus and groupthink. Christ followers should pursue unity in the church but be sensitive to the trap of like-mindedness that can sometimes be less about biblical truth and more about avoiding conflict. If everyone agrees on serious issues, that may be positive, but it may also be a sign that the group is in an echo chamber. There are certainly times when people have questions, but if they are afraid to ask them, that is a problem.

When groupthink is discussed in textbook or case studies, the construct is often portrayed from a negative perspective. This is mostly due to certain historical events, such as President Richard Nixon's White House culture, which ultimately contributed to the Watergate Scandal and the eventual resignation of the President. History has also shown us cults, authoritarian governments, and insurrectionists. Again, unity of thought is not automatically a problem. Churches, nonprofit organizations, companies, and social groups will often adopt a voluntary sense of oneness and common purpose. The primary concern is groupthink situations that are very insular, where groups have isolated their decision-making, moving from accountability and openness to preventing fresh insights from outside sources.

UNITY PAIRED WITH HUMILITY

Before we get too deep down a path of cynicism toward any group that displays even a hint of myopia and resistance to outside ideas, it is important to issue a reminder that community can be a wonderful aspect of God's kingdom. This was discussed in chapter 1. When the family of God is working together and living out a biblical calling, it can be a beautiful sight to behold and join in pursuing. The challenge is that this unity must be paired with a constant mindset of humility, self-reflection, and accountability and an external review of practices. Churches are notorious for believing that their physically open doors on a Sunday morning are more than sufficient, when in fact we need to confess our closed hearts.

From time to time, I will hear people express a version of the sentiment "I don't understand why people don't . . ." This is typically a statement of lament, as well-intentioned individuals are unclear as to why other people might view the world from a different perspective. Unfortunately, we forget that there are other ways of thinking. When people utter that specific phrase, it may also be a sign that they simply do not talk with enough people whose views are outside their circle of beliefs. If you don't understand why *people* think a particular way, perhaps you should ask one of *them* to explain their way of thinking.

It is not unusual for people to believe that they have the right perspective on the world. If I am honest, my way of thinking often (if not always) makes sense to me. The trouble comes in when we project that mindset onto others. It is not uncommon for people to conclude that, as soon as *those* other people who are all wrong discover how wrong they are, life will be good. Essentially, we hope for another *Brady Bunch*-style sitcom ending, where the antagonist of the story says "Thank you for pointing out the error of my ways to me. I will be better going forward." That does happen from time to time, but we can't treat it as a daily strategy. Also—and I hate to break this to you—*those* people may be hoping that *you* will have a similar epiphany about your wrongheaded thinking.

PEER REVIEWS

When we think through the constructs of family, friendship, educational systems, and churches, there is often a balance of challenge and support. At least there should be. That said, only you can decide how much you want those mechanisms to provide both encouragement and critique. Do we want our closest circle to consistently affirm our views and behaviors, even if we are misguided, or would it be good for them to ask us the tough questions when we make (or are about to make) mistakes? We talk about accountability on a personal and organizational level, but we often don't want to do the work ourselves. The hard questions must be asked—and, more importantly, answered. Few of us want to be critiqued. We would rather people just agree with us.

Again, we must ask whether we truly know what it is we don't know. More importantly, do we care? Typically, the more people learn, the more they realize how much knowledge is out there. This can be a daunting reality, but also exciting for those who love to explore. The key challenge is that I can't make you care, nor can I compel you to be interested in the larger world. There are plenty of people, me included, who are not interested in learning certain new things. The attitude can be that we got this far in life without new information, so there is no reason we cannot continue to function and be successful without fresh data.

There is much talk about diversity in this world, for a variety of reasons. Diversity can apply to a variety of human categorizations. Race, ethnicity, religion, and gender are common areas of diversity that are discussed in various settings. This may be a more abstract suggestion, but it is possible that diversity of thought represents the most profound aspect of human division. We do not always seek out diversity, and again, it is not always a bad thing to desire commonality with other people. Commonality can lead to shared goals, joint visions for the future, and a desire to create a better world. However, we must constantly be vigilant against prejudice and an unwillingness to venture outside our physical or ideological circle. This was addressed in chapter 5, when I talked about biases and the ways our sin nature limits our thinking; these issues in our own lives must be constantly monitored.

When people publish professional research, it is typically expected to go through a process that is referred to as peer review. In this case, peers are individuals with similar levels of education and experience who can critique the research process that was employed during the study. Obviously, people are flawed, so review by a group of peers does not guarantee an absence of mistakes. In addition, most research studies will include a section called Limitations, in which the author talks about the study having been conducted with only a narrow group of subjects. At the end of most research studies, this limitation is reiterated, and the reader is encouraged to conduct or consult many, many more studies before drawing any definitive conclusions.

Why is this important to know? When a study is reported on in the mass media, the subject matter is often simplified so that the average reader can digest the results. Unfortunately, what is often lost is the previously mentioned section on limitations, along with the urging of the researchers to avoid any assumptions that their study is anything more than a singular piece of research within a vast ocean of data. It is not uncommon for the average person to suggest that they have conducted "research," which may consist of an Internet search and a couple of confirming media sources or blogs. Put simply, those individuals did not conduct research. They confirmed preexisting beliefs with the help of an algorithm designed to return similar results based on previous searches. No peer review in sight.

ARE WE *US* OR *THEM*?

Why do echo chambers form? Oftentimes, a group may feel that there is an enemy to be defeated. Therefore, a defense must be readied. Tony Campolo, quoting Eric Hoffer, states that a movement can exist without a god but cannot exist without a devil. In other words, there must be an enemy. We see this narrative in religion, politics, and storytelling. Is this premise true? Can an ideology stand alone? Or must it always be in opposition to something? To be fair, there are enemies we must face. As mentioned above, Satan is real, and as Christians we must be vigilant. The question we must ask is whether our fellow Christian is our enemy. Satan loves a church divided. In Matthew 12, Jesus tells us that a house divided cannot stand. We may feel that we are creating unity by enclosing our community, but we may also be sowing the seeds of division or extending thick hedges between groups that might otherwise find unity through dialogue.

Regardless of our worldview, it is easy to embrace the villain construct. In the original movie *Star Wars*, Darth Vader is the clear villain. As in other stories, his role is established early, and it doesn't really matter why he is the antagonist. The objective observer would not have a hard time concluding that the Rebels could be defined as terrorists, but their behavior is excused because they have been established as the heroes of the story. Interestingly, when future movies were made that went back in time and told the story of how Darth Vader became what he was in *Star Wars*, he almost became a sympathetic figure. This is not to suggest that every villain in this world is a nice person in scary outfits that will be understood once we analyze their childhood, but it is a reminder that we don't necessarily want to ask too many questions. That requires too much thinking for some people.

There is also the common fear of the slippery slope, which in most cases is a philosophical fallacy. To be fair, change does beget change. Legal decisions are often about precedent, and future decisions are made based on what has come before. It can be difficult to change a trend that has become a standard expectation in society, but history tells us that complete reversals of seemingly fixed behaviors have changed over time. In addition, we must be aware of our own biases that lead to our not wanting change. For some change to happen, we are called to give up things ourselves that we may not be willing to relinquish.

When we have believed something for a very long time, taught it to others, and defended principles, it can be disruptive and embarrassing to consider the possibility that we might have been uninformed or misguided. There may be people who grasp that they need to change their thinking, but pride and stubbornness can keep them rooted in the group. We always see ourselves as being on the *good* side of an issue. We can point this out in others, but can we recognize it in ourselves?

Could you leave your social or ideological group? What would happen if you were to disagree with the members or leadership of your social circle? It is understandable why some questions are not asked. People who make big changes in their lives can face being ostracized. Why do people stay in bad relationships or continue to work for dysfunctional companies? For some, the prospect of being alone is worse. This may be hard for people to grasp, but a fear of starting over can be a powerful motivator to remain entrenched.

There is safety in numbers. So, where do you spend your time and energy? Guarding the walls of your ideological kingdom? Or getting out and sharing the good news?

PRACTICAL TIP

Complete the audit that was referenced at the beginning of the chapter by evaluating the demographics of your social circle. To evaluate demographics, think about (and maybe write down) a breakdown of the age, gender, race, ethnicity, economic status, marital status, geography, education, cultural background, family structure, and common interests of your most prominent social group.

DISCUSSION QUESTIONS

1. If you are honest, do you prefer to dialogue only with people who generally agree with your viewpoints and beliefs?
2. Do you believe that you exist in any sort of echo chamber? How do you know?
3. Where is the line between fostering a supportive community and limiting outside viewpoints?
4. What steps do you take to expand your perspective and limit your propensity to exclude outsiders?

9

DEFINING OUR TERMS

HONESTY CHECK

Is it possible that there are words you use on a regular basis you might struggle to define if asked?

It is possible that I may be annoying at parties from time to time. I don't necessarily go out of my way to be irritating, but at the same time I don't follow conventional wisdom when it comes to conversational protocols. Conventional wisdom suggests that a party is typically intended to be a light social event and that certain heavy or controversial topics should be avoided to maximize relaxation and entertainment. Avoiding certain topics has never been my goal at parties, nor do I think it will be in the future. I would rather have a deeper conversation, which can provide its own form of intrigue and opportunity to grow a relationship. This is not to suggest that I look for conflict, but I am more than willing to discuss religion, politics, or other complicated issues when they come up during the discussion.

Part of this strategy involves asking questions. If I am asked a question, I will sometimes answer with a question. Yes, I am that person. I can honestly state that I do not do this to be difficult. This is an intentional choice that helps with efficiency and effectiveness of dialogue. Too often a discussion begins over a particular topic, and people will bring up an oft-used word or concept. Unfortunately, the parameters of that word may be left undefined. Thirty minutes later the arguers discover that they were discussing two different topics. This can be avoided, or at least minimized, but asking a few clarifying questions at the outset of the conversation.

WORDS, WORDS, AND MORE WORDS

The word *lexicon* refers to "the vocabulary of a person, language, or branch of knowledge." This is not a particularly controversial definition, but the phrase "of a person" is particularly interesting to consider. Whether or not the definition intends to imply this conclusion, every person reserves the right to decide their own meaning of a particular word. Don't believe me? Find a culturally complicated word, ask ten people to define it, and then compile the results. If you really want to have some fun, bring those ten people together and see whether they can agree on one definition. Each one of those definitions may have an origin, but the person still will embrace their own version, both in understanding and in application.

This is another situation in which we must return to the content of chapter 5 and confront our biases. Are we willing to admit that for every term that comes across our cognitive desk, we make our own determination as to how it should be understood? This is another situation that has a major impact on our use of language and particular words. As discussed in chapter 4, words and language don't just function as identifiers of people, places, things, ideas, or actions. Language is also an indicator of culture and of how people think, which is why some words do not translate cleanly from one language to another.

We must recognize that every time we speak or listen we make assumptions about meaning. Whatever we process in our minds makes sense to us. In addition, all it takes is for one other person to agree with our definition and the stereotype is solidified. We essentially carry our own dictionary in our head, and not only are we the final authority on definitions, but those descriptions are subject to change without notice. This is not necessarily a bad thing, as new learning should result in updated understanding. The key challenge is to remain humble and consistently recognize that there is an egotism to how we process and understand the terminology of life.

AMBIGUITY EXPRESSED AMBIGUOUSLY

Ambiguity generally refers to something that can have more than one meaning. This is a normal part of language and, in many ways, general behavior. A single word can mean many things, as can a facial expression or aspect of body language. Sometimes these variations are amusing, but in other situations they can cause a level of conflict. Often ambiguity is greatly impacted by context, as well as by other words that are packaged with a particular term. When we build relationships with other people, they may become more attuned to how we understand and express language.

Let me give you a few examples. We will start out with something light. When I was growing up in the 1980s, there was a musical designation that was loosely referred to as classic rock. During that time the term broadly referred to music that debuted somewhere in the 1960s and carried until some point in the

1970s. If that definition feels to you as though several variables have been left undefined, you are right. The designations and time periods were not exact, and if someone were to ask for clarification on exact dates and musical styles, they might get a range of answers.

The term "classic rock" continues to be used today, but the timeline may have shifted, depending on who is using it. A younger person might refer to the music of the 1980s or 1990s as *classic*, even though someone my age might correct them on their designation. It is important to note that, in this example, the person using the word doesn't feel any pressure to match their definition with those of other people groups. Therefore, classic rock could truly be from two (or more) different eras since both groups of thinkers are comfortable with defining their own perspective on that construct.

To be fair, there is some subjectivity and ambiguity in life that can be difficult to avoid, and avoiding it should not be our goal. This is part of the human experience of attempting to describe our existence. Language is an incomplete mode of communication. Sometimes words get in the way of what needs to be conveyed and understood. That is why people sometimes stay silent and give a grieving person a hug. I remember a pastor once talking about the process of expressing comfort to someone else in the face of loss. He said that sometimes it is better to say "I don't know what to say" instead of trying to come up with the right phraseology that will provide an antidote to a particular situation. Sometimes words fail us, and there are times when an exact set of parameters may be difficult to achieve.

MORE COMPLICATED AMBIGUITY

More complicated ambiguities arise when we get into the nuanced and complex topics that lead to dispute and division. A good example is the designator that is often referred to as "big government," which has been used many times but is not always clear in terms of definition. The general construct of so-called big government refers to the idea of government providing certain services and enforcing regulations involving individuals and groups. This increase in relative size is financed through additional tax dollars, which further burdens the common citizen and creates layers of bureaucracy.

In a society that values the self-sufficiency of the regular person, an abundance of government oversight is unwelcome, and for most people this is not a hard argument to make. Even people who are comfortable with the government providing certain services might still agree that societal self-sufficiency is better. The difficulty is not in determining whether people would like additional freedom and less tax burden. In this case, the difficulty is ambiguity.

What is "big"? Is the government big now? If not, when will it arrive at a size at which the idea of bigness can be quantified? Is big just about a dollar amount? Or is it more conceptual in terms of the needs and wants of the individual? In other words, is the government big if regulators start to police your specific behavior or organizational life? The possibility exists that the usage of the ambiguous word *big* is not really the issue. Referring to "big government" in a negative sense might be another way of simply saying, "I don't want anyone telling me what to do, government or otherwise." That is admittedly a particular type of analysis, but we'll get back to that when we talk about red herrings.

To be fair, we have established certain measurements that are generally agreed upon in society. Tape measures. Thermometers. Speedometers. The speed limit sign posts a number instead of saying "Please drive responsibility," though it is interesting that beer ads will remind the reader "Please drink responsibly." For some people, responsible drinking consists of zero beverages, but a company would never state that because for a beer company there is value in ambiguity. When it comes to ambiguity, we must ask ourselves whether terminology can, or should, be clarified. Again, we return to various biases and to whether people can admit that sometimes their perspectives are unflinching. For some individuals the government is always too big because that is their paradigm. Others can unpack the more nuanced definitions of these ambiguous ideas.

What we also must understand and examine is the idea that definitions can change over time, either with specific actions or via more subtle shifts. While many fast-food restaurants participated in the overall increase in portion sizes over the last few decades, McDonalds is often the company that was the focal point of critique. The early McDonalds franchises did not have as many options. They sold a hamburger that is smaller than many that are sold today by various quick-serve companies. The original burger was eventually replaced by larger sandwiches on a main menu, but that original item started being served in the kid's meal. Later, that same burger was repackaged in what McDonalds called a "mini" meal.

The impact is that you have one product that is originally designated as an adult-sized entree but is later categorized as a portion appropriate for a child and is eventually described as a snack. This is a relatively minor example, but it shows how our perception can change over time. The same can be said about the size of beverages. Much as with the discussion about government, what specific quantity is designated by small, medium, large, or extra-large? Those quantities have also changed over time, and while health agencies would strongly recommend that we not consume *large* quantities of certain types of beverages, society tends to adjust to trends. In other words, if the medium beverage is of a similar size at various locations, that becomes the norm.

DIRECTIONALLY CHALLENGED

There are some similarities between vagueness and ambiguity in that both describe a lack of clarity. However, while ambiguity refers to something that can have multiple meanings, vagueness often refers to a description that lacks boundaries. If you were to ask someone how far away a destination was and they responded "not too far," you might find that answer to be a little vague. Does not *too* far mean one city block or a mile? Both are possibilities with that type of answer. If the person answering were older and leaning on a walker, you might draw a different conclusion than if they were younger and dressed in running clothes.

Since I have already introduced the awkward topics of government and politics, we might as well address the vagueness of ideology. In many countries there are defined political parties, but alongside those organizations there may also be designations of political beliefs. It is not uncommon for people to self-label or suggest that other people's political ideologies as either "left" or "right." Left or right of what? And why not up and down? Why do I have to lean in a certain direction at all? This terminology is often paired with other words, including "liberal," "conservative," and "progressive." I'll get to that in a moment.

Suffice it to say that there are problematic ambiguity and vagueness with each one of those designators. Whether we are willing to commit ourselves to the hard work of clarification is part of our daily challenge. It is reasonable to suggest that we embody a variety of vague and ambiguous designators, and it is hard to defend the idea that we are ever only one thing. The other aspect to consider in this regard is that of groups and affiliations. As discussed earlier, the individual person may often decide what a term or word means. The same goes for various groups. Again, this is not necessarily a bad thing, but it is something to consider. The size of a house matters, but location may have a more powerful influence on price.

TERMINOLOGY CHALLENGES: PUTTING PEOPLE IN GROUPS

Sticking with the political theme, let's talk about some of those terms that are used to describe certain groups. One example is the seemingly ongoing battle between the so-called liberals and their rivals, the conservatives, as mentioned above. Once again, we are faced with the difficulty of trying to define our terminology with words that have multiple meanings and complicated applications. Of course, that is assuming that individuals are interested in more specific definitions. Or, on the other hand, are they content to embrace an enemy complex prompting them to simply choose to stay at war with their ideological rival?

At face value, the term "liberal" is not necessarily a politically charged word, though that is one aspect of the definition in many dictionaries. The same can be said about "conservative." One dictionary defines *liberal* as "willing to respect or accept behavior or opinions different from one's own; open to new ideas." By itself, this doesn't seem like a terrible construct. One would think that a willingness to accept that I am not the expert on all things would be a good mindset to maintain.

In the other corner is the word *conservative*, which one dictionary defines as "tending or disposed to maintain existing views, conditions, or institutions." Again, there are a lot of positives here. If something works, why change it? What good are values if they aren't maintained over some period? Just because there is a new gadget out does not mean I have to run out and get it, particularly if the latest features do not provide a measurable level of increased productivity and efficiency.

So, where did we go wrong? Why are these people (whoever they are) at war? Don't we all embody a combination of liberal and conservative tendencies? Don't we, consistently, embrace some new ideas while reacting with skepticism toward others? The answer to these last two questions is yes and yes. We are all somewhat liberal and somewhat conservative. It just depends on the day and the issue. In addition, I may appear very conservative to some people but very liberal to others. It just depends on where I am. Also, without measurable qualifiers, certain variables will always be subjective. This suggests that there is much more going on than just two ambiguous groups of individuals who may or may not be the same collection of people. More on that in a moment.

SLANG AND OTHER VARIATIONS

There are other challenges with our terminology, and while I am unable to verify this exactly, it has been conveyed to me in the past that the English language can be difficult for people to learn. The reason for this is reportedly twofold. One, while it is probably incorrect to suggest that any language is pure and free from outside additions, English appears to be a language that is constructed from a wide variety of sources. In simpler terms, English has done a lot of borrowing. This means that the English language is not always consistent in terms of structure.

The second challenging aspect of English is the sometimes amusing but at other times frustrating construct of slang. The term *slang* refers to words or phraseology that may blend vagueness, ambiguity, and autonomous decisions to describe something in a way that in some cases appears to be truly random. Slang can be hard for people to figure out because it lacks continuity and is always changing. There are many situations in which slang terms are definitively different from another meaning of a word.

Consider the word *cool*. In practical terms, the word *cool* may be an agreed-upon way to measure temperature. The water, the surface, or my beverage is cool. Admittedly, that usage can be vague and relative to situations and interpretations, but there is still a broad consensus on meaning and a broad understanding of the word when used in a temperature-oriented context. The word *cool* can also be used in a slang situation to describe something in a positive way. Describing a vehicle as a *cool* car may have nothing to do with temperature but might instead be a way for the person to suggest that they appreciate the look.

Is it any wonder that we struggle to understand each other since words not only have different meanings but can sometimes evolve to the point that they are used in an entirely different context? The beauty and frustration of language is that it changes over time. Slang may eventually become mainstream, and dictionaries that are well regarded by society make decisions each year to add new words to their massive lists. Each new generation of young people seemingly comes up with their own slang terms, some of which carry on over a long period of time. Again, some people find this frustrating, while for others this phenomenon is amusing. What is clear is that understanding new language requires ongoing study and attentiveness to societal trends.

DEFINING A RUBRIC

One definition of the word *rubric* is "an established rule, tradition, or custom." An interesting aspect of this definition is the word *established.* As individuals and as organizations, we may at times come up with agreed-upon definitions for words, phrases, and concepts. That doesn't change the fact that words are essentially moving targets, subject to change without notice. The presence of slang shows that words can definitively change over time in meaning and usage and shift the way in which people understand myriad subjects.

We are again faced with a process of asking questions, clarifying thoughts, and writing language that can be frustrating and time-consuming. Anyone who has ever written a contract or a policy manual knows that many hours can go into specific wording and phraseology. Multiple individuals may read over the text and make suggestions so that the final product removes as much vagueness and ambiguity as possible. Granted, there is some policy that is couched purposely in vague or ambiguous language, often for legal reasons.

Would our society be a better place if a group of people were to sit down and define vague and ambiguous constructs such as "liberal" and "conservative"? Perhaps, although there would have to be agreement, not only within the group establishing the definition but also within society at large. Even if we were to establish definitions for particular words, how long would it take for us to come up with a controversial new idea that also lacked clarity?

This is where we return to the party and decide whether we are willing to clarify words with the individual who is standing in front of us. Society can change over time, but shifts often start with one conversation. As stated at the beginning of this chapter, this may include asking several questions until certain variables are established. A good example is the word *evolution*. The functional definition of the word *evolution* means change over time. Is that bad? No. And yet, there is a lot of baggage attached to the word due to its usage in science, the writings of Charles Darwin, and ongoing discussions involving the origins of the universe. While these discussions are complicated, nuanced, and require much reading, may I suggest that if someone were to ask whether you *believe* in evolution, I would urge you not to answer until you clarify the scope and definition of that word in the given context. All people believe in change over time. Not all people believe in specific amounts of change or agree on a specified period. That is the difference, but that can be explored only through clarification.

If any sort of rubric is established, are we willing to apply it to various situations? Sometime in the not-so-distant past, society was introduced to the construct of so-called "cancel culture." I wish I could give you an exact definition of this idea, but it loosely referred to groups of people protesting individuals, products, and ideas. Some of this included groups that wanted to pull down statues of controversial figures in human history or force changes to products that bore logos that were no longer considered acceptable to the public, as they may have depicted marginalized groups or offensive stereotypes.

Some segments of society lamented this so-called movement; this included Christians who worried that a secular society would change the historical record and eventually call for freedom of expression to be revoked. To be fair, Christians have organized and promoted boycotts of products, companies, and other organizations for decades. But are cancelling and boycotting the same thing? Certainly, this could be a nuanced discussion, but there are similarities between the two. The difference is that one group decided on a rubric but did not obtain agreement from another segment of society. How can this be resolved? People might have to talk it out.

WHAT ARE WE REALLY TALKING ABOUT?

As promised, let's talk for a moment about fish. Specifically, herring. Red herring. As discussed, there are literal definitions and there are conceptual constructs. A red herring can be an actual fish that people catch and eat. However, in complex conversation a red herring is defined as "a misleading statement, question, or argument meant to redirect a conversation away from its original topic." Does the terminology you are using capture the real issue? Or is it possible that there is something else going on? Remember the quote in the last chapter from Tony Campolo? If you have forgotten, the implied idea is that people tend to be enemy-oriented. There always must be someone or something that is a threat to us. It doesn't really matter what terminology is used in some situations. What is important is that there are *us* and there are *them*. Sadly, the church can embrace this mindset.

When I was in the sixth grade, our teacher had us do an exercise called Kreffles, Twits, Zoons, and Gloofers. This was a sociological exercise that was intended to expose biases and teach diversity. Each student was assigned to one of the four groups, and each group was designated as having different strengths, weaknesses, behaviors, and traits. We engaged in various projects to highlight and contrast our groups, and while it did not devolve into a *Lord of the Flies*–type situation at which we put on war paint and attempted to eliminate the other groups, there were aspects of rivalry that could have blossomed very quickly.

Ultimately, we must explore whether our thoughts, feelings, beliefs, and associations are really about words or about something else. Is a person actually a liberal or a conservative? Or are those just ways to describe whether they are part of my group or a member of the enemy tribe? As mentioned at a couple of points in this book, evil does exist. However, who is my actual enemy? Is it a nameless, faceless movement that I cannot define by membership or measurable ideology? Can I articulate the challenges of the world today because I have taken the time to study and clarify? Words matter, and they are certainly more useful when we can define them.

Speaking of clarification, do you have a plan? We will discuss that in the next chapter.

PRACTICAL TIP

When you hear a word that you cannot easily define, write it down and look it up later. See whether the stated definition matches your understanding.

DISCUSSION QUESTIONS

1. What are some terms you use that might be described as ambiguous?
2. Do you label yourself with any political, religious, or social terms? Can you quickly and easily explain what those terms mean?
3. What group of people makes you concerned? Can you measure or specifically define them?
4. What movements, ideologies, or other trends concern you? Are those measurable, and could you articulate their beliefs and overall goals?

10

WHAT IS THE PLAN?

HONESTY CHECK

Does your desired reality exist? Has it existed in the past, and if so, could you articulate the elements that allowed for it to be? What changed?

Dialogue in the church is often focused on where we are, but sometimes it is about where we are going. In a world that includes a certain number of wistful visionaries, there are some people who do not dream of bigger realities. These grounded individuals live their life, attempt to create an acceptable balance of pleasure versus pain, work to avoid major tragedies, and simply tolerate their existence. This doesn't sound very inspiring, right? For some it is enough to live a reasonably enjoyable life and not to worry about engaging in larger endeavors. I once had a student who, because he did not believe in a higher power or any sort of afterlife, described to us his eventual future. That future consisted of a bag of mulch—in other words, a literal version of "dust to dust," where he would eventually become a broken-down, simple addition to the ground. He wasn't loud or boisterous about this expected end to his existence. For him it was a very matter-of-fact reality, and he seemed genuinely okay about it. Why sweat the small stuff if your future involves fertilizing a future generation of grass? Some might find the prospect of that type of future to be a depressing thought. For this student it was freeing.

In the movie *The Big Lebowski* we are introduced to "The Dude." Without spoiling too much of the plot, I can tell you that the mantra of The Dude is "The Dude Abides." In the movie The Dude does not appear to have grand plans for his existence. He lives in his apartment, goes bowling with two friends, consistently drinks a cocktail called a White Russian, and is unemployed. The movie itself chronicles a caper that unfolds around The Dude, but his general existence does not seem to cause him any anxiety. He exists, or, more accurately, he abides. Why worry about anything bigger?

What is interesting about this film is that it has become what is referred to in the entertainment industry as a cult classic. When the movie was first released, it did not do particularly well at the box office. Like many other cult classics, over time a dedicated following of fans dragged the movie back into a niche spotlight, which has even led to books, festivals, and a website at which you can order a certificate that allows you to become ordained as a Dudeist Priest.

If we analyze the fascination with The Dude, we find an interesting life philosophy. Certainly, The Dude, if queried, might articulate a desire for peace and love for all the world. However, he does not seem to be particularly driven to pursue anything in the way of career, family, hobbies (besides bowling), or life projects. If the world is going to exist in harmony, he won't be putting forth a lot of effort toward that outcome. That lack of vision is strangely appealing to some people who may feel a desire to shed the expectation to be productive citizens who chase visions, dreams, and long-term goals.

A BIG . . . PLAN?

Before you worry that we have gone in a very different direction from what you imagined for this chapter, that introduction was written to set the stage for a contrasting viewpoint. Other people see the world very differently from The Dude. They see a particular reality that most certainly does not exist right now but is still a future that is bold and worthy of passionate pursuit. Many people have ambition, and it is obvious that they do.

As discussed in chapter 2, an *argument* may represent a verbal conflict, but it is also a word that describes your ability to articulate a position, line of reasoning, or point. In many cases, arguments and perspectives point toward a future or existence that has not yet been achieved. There is value in being a person who might be labeled as a visionary, or even a dreamer. In some cases researchers pursue a solution to a tangible problem and are fueled by the conviction that they will succeed despite all evidence to the contrary and many years of failure. What is less clear is whether people of this mindset can articulate what that world looks like to then in measurable terms.

Potter Stewart was a Justice on the United States Supreme Court. In 1964 the Supreme Court was debating a First Amendment case on pornography. At a particular juncture in the case, Justice Stewart was asked to define *pornography*. He offered the interesting, but ultimately unclear, answer of, "I can't define it, but I know it when I see it." This again returns to the challenge laid out in chapter 9 about defining terms. There is nothing wrong with sharing a conceptual idea of how you would like the world to look. However, if you can't quite describe it to people, there might be a problem in terms of implementing your vision. Or others might interpret it differently and pursue an outcome that is not to your liking.

To be fair, there are people who have certain gifts when it comes to visualization, and there are those who struggle to paint a picture. If you think about designing a building or a space, it is helpful to work with an architect. That individual may not be able to get inside your head, but they are trained to take vague descriptions and form them into a plan that is visually represented on paper. Obviously, those plans are often modified and, in some cases, simply rejected for not getting anything right. In that scenario, is it the fault of the person describing the space or the person trying to draw it without a lot of specific guidelines?

G. K. Chesterton once wrote, "It isn't that they can't see the solution. It is that they can't see the problem." With all due respect, I might suggest that some people struggle to see either of those concepts. At the end of the movie *Sneakers* (spoiler alert), the protagonists accomplish a goal that for various reasons cannot be shared with the public. To keep them quiet, they are granted the opportunity to make certain requests. One member of the group asks for a recreational vehicle. Another character asks for peace on earth and good will toward men.

It is a funny moment as the wish-granters are taken aback by this request. Conceptually we might be able to understand such an outcome on some level, but it is still very abstract. The iconic words of the song "Imagine" by John Lennon have resonated for decades, but the images remain a set of outcomes that are more constructs than measurable plans; hence the title of the song.

Whether we are talking about visions or simple dialogue, the need to articulate a measurable plan remains. Even if we utilize Socratic Seminars or other methods, people are always going to ask for a step-by-step plan. Are we able to articulate a plan to others in such a way that they can repeat it back to us succinctly and accurately?

A BOOLEAN MINDSET

For one glorious semester when I was in college, I was a computer science major. Most of that semester was spent staring at a computer screen, assembling bits of programming language that would have been a complete mystery to an outsider. Despite this reality, what the carefully constructed chains of code represented was a pathway, a roadmap for accomplishing tasks. Without these pathways, countless modern devices would only be boxes of wires and circuits.

Computer programming, along with many other decisions in life, is based on what is called Boolean logic. There are many layers of complexity, but on a basic level the logic is structured around a series of if/then statements. Think of this as being like giving directions to a particular destination. Go this direction. If you get a four-way stop, turn left. If you get to a fork in the road, curve to the right. Your destination is on your left after the red mailbox. If you get to train tracks, you have missed your destination and must turn around. Flow charts are built around these types of variables, and they are designed to direct a person along a particular path so that they choose the appropriate destination.

For some of you, this may feel a bit abstract. That is understandable, but in some ways this is a way to measure your ability to think through a process. Put another way, this is a methodology for exploring the construct of critical thinking. There may be a desired destination, but are you able to articulate a path by which it can be reached? If you have a vision for the future, can you explain how to get there in measurable steps? What happens when the steps don't work as designed?

This is also a good time to mention that the definition of the word *logic* is somewhat a matter of personal perspective. While the process described in the previous few paragraphs may be a version of logical thinking, it is still humans who plug in the variables. Much as with bias, we each have our own version of logic based on our prior experiences, knowledge, and expertise. As mentioned in chapter 7, human beings can easily assume that correlation is the equivalent of causation, and there are many flowcharts that assume relationships that do not exist. If we start down the wrong path, reaching our destination may go from difficult to impossible.

S.M.A.R.T. GOALS

There is a common mechanism that is used in business and other fields that helps people define and order their goals. This mechanism refers to S.M.A.R.T. goals, and in most cases it refers to goals that are Specific, Measurable, Achievable, Relevant, and Timebound. There are variations to the acronym, but in general terms a goal or plan should address each of the five factors. The key challenge with this or any model is that establishing these variables does not guarantee completion.

The model itself may require a certain amount of thought and discussion. The key with the Specific variable is that the concept should be easily understood by a variety of people. There must be something tangible that can be grasped so that people can capture a vision for the outcome. The Measurable establishes an expectation that achievement will be reasonably identified and recognized. Often an outcome is measurable when it is quantitative, which means that there is a number assigned to it. However, there can be other ways to verify measurability that are more qualitative in nature.

The Achievable piece can sometimes require a longer conversation. Conventional wisdom says that limited resources will inhibit the completion of certain goals. However, when it comes to faith-based conversations, this is where Christian faith and the belief in God's limitless power can play a vital role. The Relevant aspect is more subtle but vitally important to consider since it asks the question of whether a particular outcome is the right course to pursue. Finally, the Timebound element gets at the idea that successful plans will often have a schedule and due dates, so that there are an urgency and a sense of accountability.

Some models substitute Realistic for Relevant, and others use Assignable instead of Achievable. Like Achievable, there is value in remaining grounded in a sense of reality, though goal setting is often fueled by an optimism about overcoming obstacles. The Assignable aspect can be a vital part of the process based on the pragmatic need to attach specific tasks to specific individuals. Too often big goals are discussed and then never completed because everyone assumes that someone else will get the work done.

A model such as the S.M.A.R.T. goal system is not required to get things done. The broader question is whether people can articulate a measurable plan for how their viewpoints will come to fruition. It is easy to identify elements of society that people don't like or point out flaws in the current system. In addition, it is usually easy to identify where people want to go. The key challenge is to map out a plan for getting from the present to the desired future state.

Admittedly, putting together a thoughtful plan can be a challenge. Therefore, many people express what they want but are unable to move forward. In a classic *Simpsons* episode, Homer goes back to college and, after discovering that he is unprepared for the final exam, says, "I have a plan. I am going to hide behind the coats and hope that everything turns out alright." This is not an unusual situation for many people. Dialogue will not overcome all the obstacles, but this is another reason we need to keep talking.

REVISITING BIASES AND PREMISES

A few years ago I heard a commencement speech, and among other topics the speaker talked to the graduates about problem-solving. The speaker suggested that sometimes we tend toward cynicism, which can lead us to the wrong questions. Given our understanding of sin, this is understandable. The world is a dark place, and there are many reasons for lament. God can redeem anything, but the world itself is not going to heal on its own.

The challenge is our approach and sometimes our initial mindset. In this case, the speaker suggested that part of our difficulty is that we ask the wrong questions. In the Bible we are told the story of a blind person whom Jesus chooses to heal. Prior to the man being healed, the people surrounding him discuss the origin of his blindness. More specifically, they ask whether the man sinned or whether his parents sinned.

This is a predictable question, and one that we often ask in one form for another. When we encounter a challenge in the church or in broader society, our tendency can be to ask Who messed up? Whose mistakes do I need to correct? Admittedly, people do make mistakes, and there is nefarious intent in our sinful world. However, we must return to chapter 5 and ask about our biases. What flawed premises do we bring to our logic argument, which may be well-intended but ultimately put us on the wrong path?

There are many movements in the world today that work toward the correction of past decisions. Whether we are talking about energy usage, the environment, political regimes, or lifestyles, there are certain groups that constantly pursue an existence in which a prior decision will be undone. Much of this may be acceptable on some level, but are people willing to think through the planning and mindset of past generations? When groups are trying to ban certain consumer products because they negatively impact the planet, will they consider the possibility that someone may have invented that item because they were trying to solve an entirely different problem?

MOVING FORWARD, GOING BACKWARD

Here we must pause and recognize a couple of elements about the future and the past. The future is uncertain, and arguably impossible to predict in many realms. The past is gone, and while memories and history remain, our perspective is always skewed, and people can tend to romanticize certain memories. In the movie *Napoleon Dynamite*, we are introduced to a secondary character named Uncle Rico, who is convinced that if the football coach would have put him in the big game many years ago, his life would now be different. People who wear their letterman jackets to reunions may be simply enjoying memories, but in some cases they are wishing they could relive certain moments.

The question is whether we can put these thoughts and feelings in context. When I was in high school, there were plenty of moments when I was desperate to get past that phase of my life . . . because it was sixth period, and I was bored. Now, people want to go back. What do they want to reclaim? I had a very positive high school experience, and there are moments when I miss it. That said, I sense that what I miss is my freedom and limited responsibility. What I didn't have at that point in my life was much in the way of experience, knowledge, or perspective.

I am always fascinated by political campaign slogans. When Barack Obama was running for office, he utilized the simple slogan of "Hope." He did not have to specify what that meant because people who write these types of slogans know that voters will fill in the blank with their own desired outcome. The simple (admittedly not so simple) next step is to connect that concept to a candidate, and before you know it that person is elected. A concept like hope would not meet the criteria of the S.M.A.R.T. goal format, but sometimes people just want to feel a particular outcome rather than articulate it.

The same campaign momentum occurred when Donald Trump ran for office. He used the phrase "Make America Great Again," which tapped into a romanticized sense of nostalgia about what the country might have been like in the past. That slogan did not address what had made the country great, how greatness could be measured, who had done the measuring, what had caused the degree of greatness to lessen, and how that greatness was going to be achieved again the future. For supporters of Mr. Trump, the path toward greatness may have been less important than the belief that the other candidate would not be an appropriate leader. Unfortunately, when it comes to politics, there are many people who get elected (in all parties) simply by convincing a voter base that the rival candidate is a poorer choice than they are.

TIMETABLES

Speaking of the future, are you committed to your plan over the long haul? What happens if it takes weeks, months, years, or even decades to reach your goal? What if your plan will require you to convince the next generation to continue your work? There is always a question of whether we are willing to invest in processes that may not pay off during our lifetime. A good example is medical research or new forms of sustainable energy. Research can be expensive and may not lead to immediate results. Are we willing to risk our short-term resources for long-term results? Some political discussions do not go well since people would rather spend their money and time on more dependable outcomes that have a more immediate payoff.

For some people, there is sometimes the trap of waiting for the naysayers to leave or an older generation to expire. Despite the reality that the church is supposed to be a loving community that embraces all generations, some younger leaders have expressed a hope that older people will hurry up and fade away. The sentiment is that eventually these older people will die off, and then the new ideas can be implemented without resistance. The challenge is that those older people had children, and some of those children embody the basic framework of beliefs handed down from their parents. Therefore, waiting to start a project may waste time and energy that will need to be dedicated to overcoming opposition.

To be fair, there are situations in which people wait for certain elements to work out. If an employee of a company is a poor performer, that organization may take steps to remove that individual after working through a series of corrective steps. However, if that employee is a year away from retiring, a supervisor may decide that a complicated and awkward rehabilitation process is not worth the effort. The question that must be answered is whether certain elements will resolve themselves without action and whether those transactions will lead to a more viable environment for change. Again, we must be careful that we do not simply hope for an unseen resolution rather than being willing to take steps and simply move forward.

LET'S GET EVERYONE IN A ROOM

This whole book is about dialogue and the value it can be for uniting people and, in the particular context of the book, the church. This may be a juncture at which you say, "Fine, let's get everyone together and come up with a plan. We'll lay our biases on the table, talk through our paradigms, manage our emotions, define all our terms, acknowledge our various communities, and assemble a workable solution." I certainly won't stand in the way of group dialogue, and this is exactly what many people and groups do to build a strategy. That said, there are some caveats to consider.

How is this going to work? We will talk about conflict styles in chapter 12, but what is the best approach to resolving differences in life and in the church? Have you ever been in a room with a group of people trying to work everything out? It doesn't always go so well. In addition to following a model like S.M.A.R.T. goals, there may need to be a strategy on how to simply direct the conversation. Much as with other goals, there is sometimes a hope that getting all the key people in the room will magically result in a peaceable outcome.

Admittedly, this can occur. However, sometimes no one wants to start the conversation. No one is ready and willing to admit their biases or agendas. People struggle to work through a session of defining terms and ground rules. Some individuals struggle to recognize their existence in an echo chamber or admit that they are emotionally invested to the point of inflexibility. All these elements can be overcome, but, as mentioned above, this process can take some time.

WHO IS THE AUTHOR OF THIS WORK?

There are some obvious biblical truths that are repeated over and over again by pastors. We are sinners, saved by grace. We need Jesus. All that we do must be placed at the feet of Jesus, lest we allow our sinful nature to cause us to forget that God is in control. When we hear these types of constructs, we nod in agreement because they are rock solid and form the foundation of how we order our lives. If that is the case, why are these messages repeated so often? The simple answer is that we don't follow them with enough consistency.

Planning is good, and I can wholeheartedly recommend that you think hard about following many of the ideas in this chapter as you work through dialogue in the church. That said, be very careful to avoid self-praise. You may be a vessel, but you are not the author. My name may be on the front of this little book, but God is still the inspiration. This is a straightforward mindset, but it is still hard to follow. Because of sin, I always want it to be *my* plan.

James 4:13–15 invites, "Now listen, you who say, 'Today or tomorrow we will go to this or that city, spend a year there, carry on business and make money.' Why, you do not even know what will happen tomorrow. What is your life? You are a mist that appears for a little while and then vanishes. Instead, you ought to say, 'If it is the Lord's will, we will live and do this or that.'" This is echoed in the Latin phrase *Deo Volente*, which translates into English as "God willing." Amidst all our dialogue, grand plans, and desires for the future, may we be reminded that God maintains the ultimate plan for our lives and that He will reveal this plan in His time.

PRACTICAL TIP

Write out a whole plan for completing any project, large or small. Then start it!

DISCUSSION QUESTIONS

1. Do you want a new existence in society or a return to an older way of life? Can you articulate what you miss about bygone days and why?
2. If you had to write down a comprehensive plan for societal change, could you do it? What might it include?
3. Is the kind of world you desire achievable? If so, what might be a tangible first step?
4. Are you comfortable implementing plans, particularly in a group situation, or would you prefer that someone else get it done?

11

SOME THOUGHTS ON TECHNOLOGY

HONESTY CHECK

When it comes to certain types of technology, could you be described as displaying addictive behavior to any device or content?

The word *technology* can mean a lot of different things. When people hear the term, they often think of certain tools or interesting cutting-edge inventions. These aspects are certainly part of the process, but technology is not just about the latest gadgets or new products that only a few people have embraced. Technology is also about innovation and the process of getting things done. New procedures or increased efficiency can represent a form of technological advancement. This aspect is more subtle because it can't always be seen by the general population, but enhanced process is a powerful aspect of individual and organizational life.

Technology is not necessarily new, as there are situations in which prior practices or systems are rediscovered or repurposed for a different function. In a more abstract sense, someone might suggest that technology represents something that hasn't been invented or discovered yet but is still a goal a person or group pursues. There is also the suggestion that technology is about creating or fixing something that doesn't yet work properly. The solution may be regarded as technology, but again, the process may be just as important. Technology often must be similar enough to other solutions to be recognized but varied enough to differentiate the new outcome from existing solutions. That is an interesting and complicated balance.

The theme of this book is dialogue, which can foster understanding and help groups of people solve problems together. One could argue that innovations will often have similar problem-solving goals. There is the caveat that sometimes the process of trying to solve one problem creates another, even if that outcome was not anticipated. This is an unfortunate reality for all people who understandably struggle to predict the future and forecast the long-term results of their short-term decisions.

There is also the challenge of how technology (or dialogue) is used. An inventor may come up with a process or tool that is intended to solve a particular problem. Unfortunately, people have different goals, and some may use that innovation for ill intent. We have seen this throughout history, as something like heavy machinery can be used for agriculture but also for waging a devastating war. When we create a forum for dialogue, we may foster a beautiful gathering of diverse ideas that combine to form a wonderful solution and a path forward. We could also create an opportunity for a group of angry individuals to pick a fight and end up screaming at each other.

Given the circumstances of our world today, a discussion of technology could probably have occurred earlier in the book.

However, I didn't want you to get distracted. Part of the reason I didn't talk about it earlier is that technology can often focus on trends or tools. I'll talk about some of these trends in this chapter, but we can easily forget that technology itself is just an expression of many other facets of experience that plague human existence. In other words, we must be careful to not focus our blame on the latest gadget when we should look at what led to its creation. We must remember that those who fear technology may be some of the same individuals who fear change on a more general level.

HISTORICAL PERSPECTIVE

As we age, it can be a very interesting mental exercise to ponder the changes in technology during our own lifetime. Depending on a person's attitude toward life and mortality, this can be a thought-provoking activity of wonder and amazement, but on a pragmatic level it can make some people simply feel old. The question we must always ask about change is whether we perceive society to have evolved or devolved over time. When I was a youngster, my family would visit my grandparents in rural South Dakota. This was before the Internet (yes, the Internet used to not exist), and contact with the outside world was limited. The sources of external information were the landline phone, the evening news on television (watched daily), and a thin local paper. As a kid, my primary concern in the newspaper was the baseball scores from the night, even though my team was often missing because they were on the West coast and the result came in too late.

Today, that seems almost unfathomable, given the amount of instant information that is available at our fingertips. World news (including high-definition video), weather, and sports scores are at our fingertips in an instant. We can communicate with people around the globe and receive almost instantaneously documents, pictures, and videos of all they experience. Our access includes seemingly limitless databases and videos on how to build or repair just about anything. Compared to that thin newspaper and a few updates on the local news, we certainly have more options when it comes to accessing information.

At times we may ponder how technology and innovation have changed our world and how we ourselves have changed. The challenge is that our memories fade, and we can either romanticize or demonize our memories. While I remember scenes from my childhood, I am not able to recreate in my head my mindset at the time. We must also step back and recognize how small our existence is, how many other people have come and gone, and how much our society has changed over time. What seems monumental to us is a miniscule blip in the course of human history. That said, change can feel profound, particularly when we compare different eras and practices.

I'm always intrigued by the portrayal of technology in film (and in books), because such usage is risky in the sense that it quickly dates the story. What is incredibly pertinent right now can quickly become outdated, and even foreign to a future audience. The use of some-to-be-dated technology can make the content of the film seem slightly less relevant to the modern audience. The same can be said about analyzing technology in print. Therefore, we need to think more conceptually about the role technology plays and about whether the latest trend or gadget truly captures the mindset and behaviors of the era being depicted.

Are we able to put certain technology into context and realize that there have always been apprehension and misuse of new things? Are we able to differentiate between what something is designed for and how it is being used? Also, can we recognize that whatever we consider to be modern will quickly seem like ancient history to a future generation? As much as we attempt to predict what people will do, say, and think in the future, this can be a largely fruitless exercise. Put simply, we just don't know.

WHAT WAS ALREADY THERE

When we look at the world today, it is not difficult to either praise or lament new ideas, trends, and constructs like technology. The challenge is that there are times when we can't separate the advancement from the larger context or what was already in place. Are we able to remember that what is currently in place also has strengths and weaknesses? Are we able to remember the praise or lament that may have been expressed about the current norm when that norm was also a new construct? The point is that we can sometimes forget that a process of evaluation has happened repeatedly over time.

Think about the infusion of smartphones into society and the advent of text messages. There was a time when there were no cell phones or smartphones and no text messaging. The technology simply didn't exist. Over a relatively short period of years, the process called texting became an incredibly common form of communication between individuals and groups. When we think about the functional process of texting, it is interesting to ponder. Some have wondered whether a text exchange is legitimate communication, and some even lament that this is how people dialogue today. When a text exchange is a long string of short phrases and in some cases single-word answers, are those individuals having an actual "conversation"?

We can attempt to answer that type of question, but it is important to return to chapter 9 and define our terms. What is a conversation? When all people were communicating through letters, did they lament not only that there was no opportunity to dialogue back and forth or that an answer could take days, weeks, or months to arrive? Some text exchanges happen over the course of hours, but can you imagine sending a text and not receiving a response for two months? This is not to suggest that sending a text and sending a written letter are synonymous, as they are clearly different. However, they have a shared purpose of communicating from one individual to another, and when we evaluate how new ways of communicating impact society we must be willing to assess the entire process.

Obviously, there are interesting nuances to how certain technological developments impact communication. With the advent of texting and certain social-media direct-messaging tools, people can instantly connect with other individuals all around the globe. This is an incredibly useful tool, but it does not compensate for problems related to the status of some relationships. For example, one interesting feature of some of these tools is that the person sending the message can see that the person receiving the message has read it. The person sending a message is then left with an uncertainty. Will the receiver answer the message later on, or did the receiver see the message but have no intention of answering? Technology has changed the process and our expectation for a response, but the core question is still about the connection between the two people; this is true whether they are texting, seeing each other in person, or even writing handwritten letters.

UNPRECEDENTED OPPORTUNITIES TO SHARE

To be fair, there are aspects of society that are vastly different today compared to the past. If you could tell the world anything, what would it be and why? Without sounding like too much of an older person, it is interesting to note that in today's world people do have a platform that could potentially reach an incredibly broad audience. When I was a child, this would have been unlikely to happen. To be on a larger stage and reach an audience of a significant size, you would have needed to grow up and achieve a certain position in life, such as that of a politician, professional musician, famous athlete, or celebrity. Today, the so-called common person can connect with audiences that reach into the millions.

Granted, the mechanism to reach these massive audiences is accessible to large portions of the population. This means that, while everyone has a platform, the residual impact is that there is a constant barrage of millions of voices. Plenty of individuals attempt to share something profound with the world, only to be largely or completely ignored by a population that can't possibly process all the messages at the same time. There is certainly great power in the communications tools of today, but in some cases we may still have to start with our own limited and tangible social circle.

Several years ago I was at a professional baseball game, and at one point in the contest a fan ran onto the field. This fan proceeded to run a meandering route, while eluding security guards for several minutes before he was eventually caught. This happens from time to time in sports, but if you are watching the broadcast these acts won't be shown so that others will be deterred from pursuing their own moments of fame. Since I had a smartphone, I filmed this fan and posted the video on YouTube. The video quickly reached 50,000 views; while this would have been an impressive reach in comparison to the limited historical possibilities, in the world of social media that number is a small result. In addition, I could ask a more impactful question. What did I accomplish? Did I make a name for myself; share a profound message; or, as a Christ follower, advance the gospel? Probably not.

From a pragmatic standpoint we can easily conclude that there is some amazing technology in the world today and that more is coming. The fact that we can instantly talk with someone halfway around the globe is an advancement that was unfathomable just a few years ago. Unfortunately, our amazement can wane very quickly. What was once a breakthrough can quickly become commonplace. In the midst of innovation, we must also recognize that human beings remain social creatures and that people will travel to the ends of the Earth (literally) to see friends and family. This brings us to what has broadly been labeled as *social* media.

SOCIAL MEDIA

As mentioned above, the world of today provides us with platforms that can reach tens, hundreds, thousands, or even millions of people. While the people we interact with are in various physical places, the network that connects us is a vast web of wireless devices, computers, wires, and satellites. The vast scope of the wiring that runs around the globe is almost beyond our comprehension, but that has become the benchmark for how we communicate.

This may be an odd way to think about social media, but picture yourself in an enormous gymnasium. You have a microphone, and there are microphones all around the room (along with pictures of emojis). You make a statement, and someone comes to the microphone and makes a comment. After that there may be others who make comments or hold up emoji signs. Of course, there are those who will say nothing. Did they hear (or in this case see) what you said? Do they care?

The interesting psychology of social media is that it creates an instant feedback mechanism and, depending on the issue, a very quick affirmation cycle or echo chamber. You post some piece of your worldview, a bunch of people affirm what you wrote, and your viewpoint gets strengthened because your network confirmed what you already knew. This is also why some people avoid serious issues altogether, and especially via email or social media. Despite the positive aspects of affirmation, there is also the risk that someone might disagree. Someone in that gigantic gymnasium might step up to the microphone and tell you that your viewpoint is misguided. Because of the forum, this pushback has the potential to be seen by all your family, friends, and the broader network. This type of scrutiny is something many choose to avoid.

Admittedly, I have been one of those individuals who is comfortable discussing difficult topics in cyberspace. I've had people say to me, "I enjoy your discussions, but I don't dare participate." They go on to explain that the environment is too intimidating and that there are too many intellectual heavyweights. That is understandable to an extent, though I always encourage people to conquer their fears and boldly share their beliefs. Technological forums can be difficult places to argue with people, particularly when networks cross and you can easily end up dialoguing with a total stranger you can't see.

This is where we must recognize that, while technology can provide pathways for bringing people together, it can also be a catalyst for division. One image that becomes part of the vernacular is the idea of someone being a keyboard warrior. The concept is that someone can slay intellectual dragons and write powerful narratives with their mighty (and sharp) computer keyboard. For better or worse, technology allows us to have an instant platform. The analogy of the gymnasium is limited because, in a practical sense, if you wanted to assemble your network in a physical space, it would take time and energy. Some people wouldn't be able to come because they are geographically far away. With social media, you get excited or upset about something and you instantly have an outlet that reaches directly to your network on their devices.

Social media can foster dialogue, and we are able to build and rebuild connections to people when this might not have been practical in the past. At the same time, there are studies linking social media use to depression. Humans are designed to interact with one another, and social media can actually increase the divide. Before the Internet we weren't sure whether our friends were having fun without us. Now we know, because there are pictures and videos, . . . and we aren't in them. For young people as well as adults, social media can provide a platform for viewing other people's lives, while we sit on the sidelines and are not asked to participate.

UNDER THE SURFACE

As discussed, we can focus our energy on blaming the technology. Obviously, the tools play a role, but we do well to bear in mind that social media did not create conflict between people. Anger, frustration, isolation, loneliness, and conspiracy theories existed long before we had the digital tools to express them to others. Our digital communication networks may have simply brought deep-seated differences to the surface that might actually have existed for a very long time.

The interesting sociological reality is that social media and other digital technology can close the gaps between people while also magnifying ideological divides. I mentioned keyboard warriors in the prior section. These warriors can defend impenetrable worldview kingdoms while gathering followers for battle and engaging in daily digital skirmishes across platforms. From a physical standpoint, we can do the same thing in churches. Not only is it possible that we are just down the street from the person we are interacting with online, but we might also see them across the sanctuary on Sunday.

There is also the interesting phenomenon of anonymity in online spaces. There are many networks that are personal and include real names and profile pictures. There are other networks that allow for people to use made-up names. I remember one student I had many years ago whose online name was Angry Potato. There are obviously some advantages of anonymity. Whistleblower laws and people who genuinely fear for their physical safety because they are in an abusive situation are good examples of the need to protect identity. However, there is also the reality that some hide behind an anonymous name because they fear conflict or don't want to face the challenge of defending their beliefs.

Do you say things to people online that you wouldn't say to their faces? Truthfully, some would. Some people are grumpy everywhere, and it didn't take the Internet to bring out their negative outlooks on life. Rudeness is also not new. People of a certain age can remember what happened when individuals had a conflict on a phone call. Not only did some people hang up on the other person, but they slammed down the handset on the receiver. This is yet another example of how technology may have changed, but people getting into an argument is nothing new. Despite the lack of a heavy handset, people can (and do) still hang up on others.

Conflict due to technology is not a new idea. As mentioned, we must recognize that the word *technology* does not apply just to the latest gadgets but to the processes and ways by which we approach decision-making. We can sometimes focus on certain tech solutions and assume they are game changers without recognizing that prior generations were also impacted by changes in communication, information distribution, and conflict resolution. Have technology and something like social media heightened the tension? Perhaps. At the same time, it is still just a forum. As with any innovation, we must evaluate how we are using what we have created.

WHERE ARE WE GOING?

Not so long ago, I posted this on a social media site: "Do you really want the world to change? Are you willing to work through complicated conversations with people who think differently from you? Do you have the capacity and, perhaps more importantly, the willingness to actively listen and allow for the possibility that your current beliefs are well-intended but possibly misinformed or incomplete? If you are honest, do you prefer to talk with people who agree with your viewpoints and reinforce what you already believe? These are somewhat rhetorical questions, but I would love some honest, transparent answers."

Posting something online does not solve the problem. A post may be the beginning of a conversation, but it is certainly not the end. In 2020 the world entered a pandemic, whose measurable end time and long-term impacts may never be fully understood. Because of technology, many people had the ability to stay connected during that time through video conferencing and other digital devices. I've often wondered how we might have handled that event if it had occurred thirty years earlier. We would not have had as many communication tools, but would we have handled the situation better or worse? That is hard to unpack.

As we move ahead, I've often wondered if we will ever create a technology that will allow people to feel as though they no longer need to meet in person. Some of the virtual reality and augmented reality devices are fascinating and powerful. There may be a time when we can put on a headset and be instantly transported to anywhere in the world. We may have the ability to walk around a space, and perhaps new innovations will allow us to engage with smells or other stimuli that engage our senses.

The question is, do we want that? Do we want to reach a point where we can sit on our couch and engage with the entire world while truthfully engaging with no one? We remain face-to-face individuals. With all the technology at our disposal, people of all ages still get together on a regular basis. Young people who are constantly on their devices still want to hang out with their friends in person whenever they can. I will dialogue with people online and am not afraid to delve into complicated topics, even though the platform can be limiting in terms of tone, emotion, facial expressions, and body language. However, there are times when I say "Let's go get coffee." A face-to-face conversation still has no substitute.

If you think about it, we could skip all family reunions, in-person meetings, dinners, and dates going forward. Travel is not necessary, and we could just use video technology. However, that is not satisfying for humans. Rather than continuing to post, post, and post some more, pick up the phone. Set up a face-to-face video conference. Go out for coffee. Go for a walk. Admittedly, face-to-face interaction can be time-consuming. We must set up an exact time, use resources to walk or drive to a location, and then focus on just one person or group. This is inefficient and yet so vital to a process of ongoing dialogue.

Ultimately, technology is very important, and it can definitively shape human existence. At the same time, it is important that we put changes in perspective. The latest gadget or craze may become a trend, or it may fade as quickly as it skyrocketed to stardom. There is a balance between nimble adaptation and patient evaluation. In addition, technology cannot overcome some obstacles and impasses that we will discuss in the next chapter.

PRACTICAL TIP

Write a letter or postcard to someone, put a stamp on it, and stick it in the mailbox. Schedule a time to have coffee with someone you haven't seen in some time. Do it right now.

DISCUSSION QUESTIONS

1. What do you think of when you hear the word *technology*?
2. Do you dialogue with people differently when you use certain types of technology?
3. Do you think that technology has had a net positive or net negative impact on how people interact over time?
4. When you think about the future of technological communication, are you more prone to excitement or apprehension?

12

IMPASSES, DETOURS, AND LETTING GO

HONESTY CHECK

Do you like to win, no matter the cost? Or are you more prone to running from a fight?

I hate to say this, but sometimes dialogue doesn't work very well, or there is a very long road to getting anything accomplished. Obviously, that is not the core message of a book on pursuing conversation, but if you have read this far you have probably grasped that there are some challenges to overcome. Our core difficulty remains the sin nature of people, and that includes me and you. Even if we pursue seemingly rational and reasonable processes of dialogue, there are going to be some challenges.

I've been a sports fan my entire life, and, as a native of Seattle, our collective trophy case has not been particularly full. That's a nice way of saying that the Seattle teams have lost a lot. In competitive sport, there are almost always a winner and a loser. In some ways, the drama and storylines between the winner and a loser are what make the contest interesting. I was listening to a sports radio program, and the host of the show was lamenting about a particular sports league and how, in his opinion, the athletes are too nice to each other. As in, "How dare they get along?" The host waxed poetic about the good old days when certain marquee franchises would play in the playoffs, all the while hating each other. That is an interesting sentiment, as though it is unacceptable for people to engage in a competitive event and still like each other on a personal level when it is over.

There are times when we take this mentality into our various communities, including the church. We may not realize how society impacts us, but if we think a "winner take all" attitude is relegated to the sports-watching part of our brain, we may want to reevaluate. When you are an athlete on a competitive sports team, you have a goal of prevailing over your opponent every single day. For nonathletes, there can still be a similar sentiment even if your workplace is not a field or court. While there is value in being ready to defend our principles, we must be careful that we aren't tempted to always have a competitive spirit that plans on impasses. There will be differences that are hard to resolve, but sometimes we will simply encounter detours on our way to resolution. In addition, there will be times when we may need to let some things go.

I MUST LOVE THESE PEOPLE?

In Matthew 10:34–39 Jesus says, "Do not suppose that I have come to bring peace to the earth. I did not come to bring peace, but a sword. For I have come to turn 'a man against his father, a daughter against her mother, a daughter-in-law against her mother-in-law—a man's enemies will be the members of his own household.' Anyone who loves their father or mother more than me is not worthy of me. Whoever does not take up their cross and follow me is not worthy of me. Whoever finds their life will lose it, and whoever loses their life for my sake will find it."

These are tough words to read, particularly if we like our family. How can loving our family be bad? To be fair, I will propose that the passage is not saying that loving family is not biblical. Nor is it suggesting that God wants everyone to be in a constant battle with one another. The passage simply lays out the reality that following Christ is an all-in commitment and that this may cause friction, even with our closest human relationships. The passage acknowledges that people can have extremely strong ties to their family and that those can be hard to leave behind when choosing contradictory ideologies and lifestyle decisions.

I will also suggest to you that the Scripture is not telling us that we cannot talk to our parents, siblings, or children once we establish a committed relationship with Jesus. Far from it. Our family may be the very people to whom we minister first. The Scripture is about priorities and how we think through our purpose as grateful children of God. I appreciate the motto of Azusa Pacific University (APU), which is "God First." In a world filled with complex ideas, sometimes we need to keep it simple and constantly be reminded who is on the throne.

This perspective also applies to our viewpoints. God first, before our politics; familiar social views; family obligations; worldly interests; carnal human desires; and yes, traditional church practices. A similar perspective is expressed by the film series *I Am Second*. While this may seem like essentially a derivative of the APU motto, there is a subtle but vital difference.

The film series emphasizes not just a position but also an attitude of humility and service. Our needs and wants are not the priority, and humility should be a constant pursuit. In addition, we aren't just second; we are a distant second. Perhaps we should assume that our place is even farther down the list.

A SENSE OF DETERMINATION

The functional challenge of any difficulty or project is knowing how much time, energy, and resources to spend on overcoming obstacles to achieve our desired result. We like the idea of challenges, but oftentimes we don't go much beyond the concept stage because we quickly realize the commitment that is required. It is hard to climb a mountain when you are out of shape and don't even own a good pair of hiking boots. Can those challenges be overcome? Absolutely. Do you want to overcome them? Only you can answer that question. When we think about dialogue, we must acknowledge that we do have limited time in life. Patience and perseverance are wonderful traits, but should we spend hours, days, weeks, months, and years on working with one person? Perhaps that is our calling, but there are times when we may need to pause and reevaluate the likelihood of change.

This isn't to suggest that we should drop a challenge at the first sign of difficulty. Author Carol Dweck talks about the idea of having a growth mindset. This isn't simply a positive attitude and a belief that things can be accomplished, though that is part of the process. Growth mindset also includes a plan or strategy on how to accomplish certain goals. This construct is often paired with the idea of grit, which is typically measured by how well people can overcome obstacles and detours. Returning to the example of computer science, if one piece of code was wrong, the whole plan fell apart. How adaptable are we when our strategy does not unfold as planned? Can we adjust? Will we overcome obstacles and keep at it, even in the face of discouragement and failure? We can apply the same mindset to dialogue. This does not necessarily mean that we pursue a singular mindset of *winning*, but it may require a more strategic approach.

We can return to the Chesterton quote in chapter 10. As a reminder, he said, "It isn't that they can't see the solution. It is that they can't see the problem." When there is an impasse in conversation or dialogue, are we able to deduce the reason? Perhaps it is the difficulty of the content, the style of dialogue, or the personalities involved. Again, in some cases an impasse is a clear sign that conversation should be abandoned. In some situations that may be a wise course of action, but how committed are we to thinking about how the difficulty came about in the first place?

Returning to sports, it is often interesting to see how TV networks will capture the moments after a major championship is won. Most of the camera time is spent on the winner, but inevitably we will see the loser, and they will be upset. We, the audience, are essentially told, "This is the winner, and this is a loser." One must wonder at that moment if the network believes that the result is unclear, given the fact that one team is running around celebrating and the other team is walking off the floor with their heads down or sitting on the bench with towel over their heads to hide the tears of utter sadness. Is this what the world is supposed to be? Does there always have to be a clear winner and a loser? Is there nothing in the middle?

CONFLICT STYLES

Whether or not we realize it, we can tend to have a favorite or most comfortable style or approach when it comes to conflict of various kinds. Some of this approach is subtle, but there are ways to establish patterns or evaluate consistent behaviors. Much as with other topics in this book, understanding your conflict style requires a level of self-reflection and honesty. There are many situations in life when we feel as though we are supposed to act a certain way. Whether we act that way or not involves more complex self-awareness. According to a construct called the Thomas-Kilmann Conflict Mode Instrument (TKI), there are five types of reactions people have when faced with conflict. Those reactions are accommodating, avoiding, collaborating, competing, and compromising.

Accommodating: The accommodating style is often about thinking of others first. Sometimes this involves a cheerful attitude, and sometimes we begrudgingly give in to people. Truthfully, it isn't always bad to be accommodating, but there are times when people are dominated by other styles and feel compelled to give away everything rather than engaging in conflict. Is a servant attitude a version of being accommodating? At times, yes. However, there are limits.

Avoiding: Some people hate conflict and will avoid it at all costs. Period. They will walk away, change the subject, and encourage people not to talk about the issue. These are the people who avoid complex discussion on social media, ask the family to not talk politics with Uncle Earl at Thanksgiving, and are quick to suggest peace when conflict arises. John F. Kennedy, quoting Franklin D. Roosevelt, once said, "The only thing we have to fear is fear itself." If we adapt that phrase to conflict resolution, some people are just afraid of the conflict; the topic may be irrelevant.

Collaborating: This is the style that many people claim to be their favorite, but results can be hard to come by. Collaboration is a wonderful pursuit, but are there ever solutions that meet everyone's needs? Sometimes, but certainly not often. The reason that some of our issues are polarizing is that they are more binary issues, which means there isn't a middle ground. In addition, there is often a need for discussion because people approach things from different angles. Coming out with a solution that makes everyone totally happy is possible, but rare.

Competing: Some people love to win, and this applies to absolutely everything. Board games, heavy discussions, and business ventures are all approached with a conquering attitude. People who are competitive will sometimes end up in sales, which can be both a blessing and a curse, depending on the industry and the tactics required to meet quotas. Some people recognize their need to compete, and they will avoid the family card game if only to spare the feelings of the people they love.

Compromising: Much of life is a compromise of different desires. We aren't always happy about it, but sometimes we are forced or feel compelled to split the difference. We would truthfully like the whole pie for ourselves and would prefer not to share. For the sake of reality, we settle for a piece. Many people go into negotiations with a desired outcome and a more reasonable result in their minds. In other words, people will identify what they want, what they think they can get, and what they are willing to accept.

This may be a helpful construct to this mechanism, but the caveats is that this is a theory. Everyone utilizes all of these approaches to a certain extent, depending on the situation and environment. No one reaction is necessarily the best or the worst way to handle things. As mentioned, at face value we may prioritize collaboration as the ideal, but oftentimes it is also the hardest to achieve. Like anything, conflict style comes down to how tied you are to an issue or outcome.

There is one more sports connection to consider. I've always wondered whether there are professional athletes who don't worry much about winning championships. You can't get to the professional level without having a degree of competition, but do some athletes simply recognize that they are privileged to play a kid's game as an adult and make a lot of money doing it? Do they feel an internal pressure to build a rivalry with someone else and have a strong sense of animosity toward other players and teams? As discussed earlier, some people don't have grand ambitions for their life. They are content to float through life and enjoy what they can. Therefore, some of those individuals are not necessarily avoiders of conflict. They just don't care that much, so they are willing to let deeper discussions pass them by.

DEFENDING PRINCIPLES OR PLAYING DIRTY?

There are times when you decide to pursue dialogue with someone, but, unfortunately, it doesn't go particularly well. This creates a sense of awkwardness and uncertainty as to how to move forward. Unfortunately, there is the hard reality that some dialogue leads to rifts, feuds, and estrangement. This was discussed in chapter 1, and in some ways this leads to people feeling afraid to pursue conflict. People are afraid that there may be a disagreement, which will lead to bad feelings and broken relationships. The alternative for some people is to keep everything on the surface and avoid the depth of relationship that could lead to disagreement.

There is obviously a balance, and this is where we again must ask whether an issue is truly important. On the one hand, many would suggest that we should maintain respectful dialogue. This is contrasted with the oft-used quote that bad things will continue to happen because good people do nothing. At what point do you say, "I just think you are wrong about this," particularly if you know that might spark a hard disagreement?

I once knew a college student who had a very public altercation with a professor. After a video-based class presentation, the professor went through a process of feedback. This dialogue eventually segued into the professor sharing some personal views on the presented subject. The student objected, and after a couple of minutes of conflicting points, the conversation ended. After class, the student uploaded the conversation to social media and sent it to a mainstream media outlet. The issues covered in the presentation and the subsequent debate between professor and student had recently been debated in broader society, so several media outlets picked up the story. Soon a video clip that had started in a classroom was streaming around the country. In the days following, the student received a fair amount of praise from like-minded thinkers.

One could argue that the student in question stood up for his principles. The difficulty is that his tactics included the use of slanted media coverage. The networks that picked up the story were media outlets that were well known for partisan reporting. The coverage included a lot of name-calling, fallacies, and labels that would not pass the expectations laid out in chapter 9. Despite that, this is how the conflict played out. The student shared his version of the truth, and he did it loudly. The professor was publicly crucified by several media outlets. Again, some would argue that real issues can sometimes require strong messaging, which is true. In this case, the gap between certain groups only widened.

THE SHORTCOMINGS OF DIALOGUE

At one point in the movie *An Ideal Husband*, a character says, "She talks more and says less than anyone I know." What we take from this is that talking is not always a productive exercise for resolution and ideological unity. Sometimes the air is just filled with words, and people don't get very far in achieving harmony. There does come a point when most aspects of an argument have been addressed but forward movement has not been achieved. When that occurs, the people engaging may need to regroup or decide that an impasse has been reached.

As discussed earlier, sometimes we use the phrase "agree to disagree." For some, there is still a commitment and willingness to keep talking. For others, this phrase means that they have tried and that is the end of the discussion. Whether individuals in that situation are willing to evaluate what they agree on and restart from there depends on the people involved. In addition, there is the question of whether one person will wait for the other party to reengage or whether they will be the one to restart the conversation. Individually, we all must ask questions when it comes to impasses and detours. How quickly do you throw in the towel? How long do you debate? How many times do you go back and attempt dialogue again? Rationally, there may be limits that are addressed in conflict resolution textbooks, but sometimes God puts people on our hearts who do not necessarily seem "worth" the effort.

When I think about this scenario, two people come to mind. One is a person I met many years ago. He is closer to the age of my parents, has lived a checkered life, and got connected to me through my church. I spent countless hours on the phone with him, listening to him talk through his anxieties and his demons. Truthfully, I don't know how much progress was made. I was a listening ear, and the relationship was very one-sided. We do not have much of a relationship today. The other person I think of is a good friend of mine, and we don't agree on much when it comes to theology and politics. At times we have probably each concluded that the other is a lost cause. Despite that, we continue to talk and support one another in brotherly Christian love. That gives me hope.

There are a few who have refused to have a conversation with me over a cup of coffee, and that makes me sad. Perhaps they are afraid, and perhaps they are stubborn. A couple of people may not have directly refused but have consistently ignored my requests to meet. I must allow for the possibility that their refusal has something to do with my personality and my way of approaching complex issues. In other words, maybe they just don't like me very much and don't really want to spend time with me. As much as we may think we are reasonably pleasant to be around, others may not draw the same conclusion.

What we always must remember is that dialogue is a combination of content and style. An oft-quoted verse is Proverbs 27:17, which says, "Iron sharpens iron, so one person sharpens another." The verse is often used as an example of accountability and how Christ followers need to create an environment in which they speak the truth in love but don't shy away from correction. What people often forget is that iron can be a rough metal—and that iron sharpening can be a definitively grating process. People may want it to be like a nice, smooth pair of shiny scissors. The problem is that when scissors gets old, it gets dull. At that point the scissors may still go through the action of cutting, but it doesn't effectively do the job. The same goes with iron sharpening iron. Are we pretending to hold each other accountable through dialogue, or are we just going through the motions?

HOPE

From time to time I've heard older couples tell their stories of how they met, fell in love, and ultimately made their relationship last. Sometimes those stories include an element of pursuit, which is a nice way of saying that one person was annoying and wore the other person down over time. Requests for dates were refused, or one half of the couple initially showed little to no interest in a relationship. This led to ongoing persistence and, eventually, a match. The stories are cute, and we like them. There are other stories of pursuit that are less fun. Someone asks a person out. They are refused. The person asks again. They are refused again. This can get awkward very quickly. Do we appreciate tenacity and perseverance? Absolutely. However, in dating and in many other societal areas, no means no. That's it. Let it go. Step away. Move on. What is unclear is when we should keep pursuing dialogue or when we should realize that our pursuit is no longer admirable.

Sometimes this realization comes from within, and other times it comes from the iron sharpening iron. Sometimes our internal and external messages are in sync, and other times they are not. In the movie *Wayne's World* we are introduced to Wayne, who among other things desires an expensive electric guitar that is prominently displayed in the window of a music store. He regularly stops by the store to admire the guitar, despite the feedback from his best friend, Garth. At one point Garth says, "Stop torturing yourself, man; you'll never afford it. Live in the now!" What is Wayne's response? He says, "It will be mine. Oh yes. It will be mine." Sometimes we label a behavior as obsession, and sometimes we call it tenacity. Spoiler alert: Eventually, Wayne gets the guitar.

My view may seem clichéd, but I must believe that dialogue can occur, that people can grow together, and that change can happen. This is where we test whether we truly believe in the power of the Holy Spirit. People can change. Stories of amazing redemption are possible. My wife has told me many times that I have an unquenchable belief that people can be reasoned with and guided to a particular conclusion. That is mostly a compliment, but my wise wife has also suggested at times that I need to let people go. Perhaps it is inaccurate to suggest that we are giving up. Sometimes we simply must hand people over to the Holy Spirit. Keep in mind that accepting that God is in control does not exempt us from doing the work.

Perhaps this is misguided optimism, but maybe it is just the idea that change can happen. As an educator, I am tasked with facilitating knowledge or, at minimum, building on it over time. I must believe that anyone can learn anything, despite ample evidence to the contrary. The work may be hard and take time, but growth can always occur. Admittedly, there are some difficult breakpoint issues. Sometimes people follow the S.M.A.R.T. goal criteria in terms of structure, but that doesn't make the issues any easier to resolve. In the final chapter we will talk about how all of this is a work in progress.

PRACTICAL TIP

Make a list of your "nonnegotiable" topics or beliefs and specify why each is on the list. Make a list of your "negotiable" topics and why each of them is on the list. Find someone who disagrees on one of your non-negotiables and have a conversation (they shouldn't be hard to find).

DISCUSSION QUESTIONS

1. Are you comfortable disagreeing with people? If so, how often and for how long?
2. When do you know when you have reached a point at which resolution seems impossible?
3. Are you prone to resorting to agreeing to disagree, and what is your criterion or timetable for using that phrase?
4. What practices have you used in the past to maintain a relationship and continue dialogue even when topics and conversation have gotten awkward?

13

A WORK IN PROGRESS

HONESTY CHECK

Will you commit to pursuing productive dialogue with everyone?

If I am honest, there are times when I get tired of talking to people and encouraging dialogue between those espousing competing ideologies. Thankfully, these moments of frustration do not happen often, but conversational fatigue is real, and there are moments of discouragement. I mentioned earlier that I have engaged in many online conversations over the years. Before I post something, particularly on a serious topic, I will read it more than once. Sometimes I pause and ask, "Should I even post this at all? Should I just let people be people? Is this worth the stress of possible conflict, which could lead to misunderstandings and difficult relationships?" The answer, still, is yes. Not only is it a good idea to foster dialogue, particularly in the church, but we are commanded to love one another. We cannot love on the surface only. If we aren't willing to have deep, meaningful relationships in the church, then why are we even here? How can we call ourselves a community if we don't talk beyond the basics of polite topics?

Because of the challenges associated with dialogue, there are times when I feel like giving up on pursuing greater understanding between different groups. The work is hard, people are stubborn, and sometimes it feels as though dialogue takes way too much time. Sometimes it is easier to just work with a small group of like-minded people and shut out the rest of the world. We have seen people pursue this strategy often, and while it can streamline some conversations while avoiding conflict, it does not often provide solutions that go beyond a very narrow criterion.

Are we doing better as a society today than we have in the past? Or, more to the point of this book, as a church? Is there evidence that we are moving forward as the church or building a closer, more Christlike community? Sin remains, so theologically it is always difficult to suggest that we are making measurable progress toward redemption. However, we are called to keep working hard in the family of God. I shared this passage earlier, but again, as James 4:14 reminds us, "Why, you do not even know what will happen tomorrow. What is your life? You are a mist that appears for a little while and then vanishes." In other words life is short, but there is work to do while we are around. Let's get to it and keep at it.

EVERY NEW DAY IS A POSSIBILITY

Probability is a concept that is studied in statistics; it utilizes mathematics to provide mechanisms for predicting patterns. In various societal realms, we use these cognitive tools to predict certain possibilities, based on many variables. While probability may guide our decisions and help us make choices, numbers do not change the fact that we have hope. Hope is a beautiful aspect of human existence, but there is a line between what is possible and what is statistically likely.

Many people play the lottery on a regular basis, and they simply shouldn't. Statistics would say that this is always a poor idea, as there is a relationship between poverty and playing the lottery. It is interesting to note the motivation that leads to our making decisions about eventualities that are not likely to occur. If there is even a remote chance of something happening, we will sometimes give it a shot, particularly if the possible reward is great.

In simple terms, we still hold out hope, and we should. It just might happen. If I keep working at it, maybe I will get through. Admittedly, there can be a difficult balance between optimism and realism. Remember the Jack Sparrow example from earlier? It isn't that some outcomes are impossible. Instead, they are im*probable*. Some conversations may be difficult, but favorable outcomes are possible. So, is world peace possible? Sure. Yes. Probable? Uh . . .

WHERE DO YOU WANT TO BE IN FIVE YEARS?

In professional settings, people are often asked a range of questions during job interviews. One common question is "Where do you want to be in five years?" Perhaps a five-year timetable is not appropriate for every decision, but there is value in imagining a more inspiring future. The challenge with a longer timetable is that it may allow us to procrastinate and minimize a sense of urgency. This is where we can return to the S.M.A.R.T. goal framework, along with a growth mindset. The key question to ask is What role will you play in pursuing this outcome right now?

As mentioned in chapter 10, the achievable or attainable part of S.M.A.R.T. goals is an interesting quandary. The same could be said about the so-called realistic aspect. What if what we want to accomplish is outside the boundaries of practicality? What role do our faith and the power of the Holy Spirit play in what we want the church to look like in the future? We love the big story of overcoming odds, and while our sinful brains tell us to manage expectations, Scripture tells us that God is sometimes about unfathomable and inconceivable outcomes.

Besides the practicality of goal setting, there is the idea that we can easily forget the past and assume that our new reality is different. T. S. Elliot once wrote a poem "Little Gidding," which included the following:

> We shall not cease from exploration
> And the end of all our exploring
> Will be to arrive where we started
> And know the place for the first time.

Poetry can have many meanings. What I take from this oft-quoted section is that our meanderings can lead to places that seem new but have in reality only been forgotten. In the context of this book, that means we can have no benchmark for progress unless we take stock of where we have been and where we might be going in the future.

LIFELONG LEARNING

When someone says that something is a work in progress, it can seem as though we are resigning ourselves to not really getting anywhere. That can be true in some situations, particularly if there isn't a measurable goal or timetable. Labeling something a work in progress can also acknowledge that some of our endeavors will continue for the rest of our life. Being a lifelong learner means just that, and we must be committed to an ongoing lifestyle of challenge and pursuit.

Along the way we must hold things somewhat loosely and constantly evaluate what is important to us. It is good to make plans, but we must also remember that we are flawed creatures who may have come up with a strategy that is based on our own needs, wants, and desires. Following the will of God can never be about ourselves, as it is always about surrender. God has the ultimate plan, and while we may construct earthly goals, we must always filter those outcomes through Scripture, along with bathing the process in prayer.

As we continue to learn, we must remember chapter 9 and realize that learning new words and terminology is also a lifelong pursuit. We must be committed to a process of etymology, which means that we seek to understand the origin of not only words but also processes and history. The study of history is complicated, and while people may debate the exact details of certain events, the hardest part of studying history is understanding what people were thinking in a past time. Whenever we consider what people were pondering in the past, we think about those issues through our own filter. That may ultimately be misguided.

One other aspect to remember as we commit to a lifelong process is that we may be prone to wanting other people to do the work. It is very easy to say that other people *should* do something. *Should* is a very powerful word, but it makes a lot of assumptions. Why should they? Lament is part of human existence, but simply complaining that life is not unfolding as we think it should because other people are not doing things does not accomplish very much. We must ask what our role will be in making the world a better place.

A NOTE ABOUT PRESENTATION SKILLS

A work in progress is a shared process that must be embraced by a critical mass in any community if traction is going to occur. Leadership certainly plays a role, and sometimes we may be tempted to bring in an individual who can inspire the community and get people excited about a vision. There are positive aspects to the strategy. I have worked with people over the years who are genuinely likable and have an authentic charisma. This can contribute to their effectiveness as a leader. Enlisting those types of leaders can be a wise decision when it comes to spearheading an initiative.

Keep in mind, though, that there are other emotions that can also act as persuasive elements, including coercion, intimidation, and blackmail. Theorists John French and Bertram Raven came up with a construct they called the Five Bases of Power, which included Legitimate, Reward, Expert, Referent, and Coercive. As with any theory, each of these aspects has pros and cons.

Legitimate power generally refers to leadership positions, as in people who have the authority to supervise or make decisions. Reward power speaks to the idea that some people can grant incentives, while others cannot. Expert power gets at the idea that some people have certain skills or knowledge that make them a helpful resource. Referent power suggests that some people are naturally respected for their presence or decision-making ability, even if they do not possess a title. Coercive power is built around a construct of imposing will, which can include various forms of punishment.

When it comes to our goals of promoting dialogue in the church, our strategy may mix some of these bases. Admittedly, the Coercive element is probably not the strategy we want to use, as punishment rarely leads to a positive outcome, particularly when promoting an exciting vision of unity in the church and further pursuit of God's kingdom. However, the rest of the power bases may have different levels of value, depending on the situation and context.

My wife and I have taken prospective students to visit and evaluate our college alma mater. People know we like the school; otherwise, we wouldn't show it. We also want to introduce the students to the idea of traveling out of state for school, even if they don't pick our favorite. We intentionally do not sit down with the students and do a hard sell, even though we have an emotional (and criteria-based) attachment to the institution. We play the role of getting them there. We may schedule certain activities, but the school must sell itself. We must keep the same mindset when presenting our vision on an issue to others and beware the lure of charisma to get us to the "next level."

STILL ABOUT HARMONY

Amidst our quest for dialogue, we must keep a hope for harmony in the back of our minds. The pursuit of conversation, particularly around complex topics, will inevitably lead to some level of conflict. Whether anticipated or experienced, those differences of opinion can sometimes cause us to forget that we are ultimately seeking to grow a more robust, genuine community.

We are enjoined in Romans 12:16–18 to "Live in harmony with one another. Do not be proud, but be willing to associate with people of low position. Do not be conceited. Do not repay anyone evil for evil. Be careful to do what is right in the eyes of everyone. If it is possible, as far as it depends on you, live at peace with everyone." All throughout the New Testament letters to the new churches, the apostle Paul constantly preached a message of tenacious faith, while also reminding people that they are part of a larger church family.

Again, the caveat is that a desire for harmony does not mean that we avoid conversation. That can also be a temptation, as we may presume that peace is achievable only through silence or avoiding awkward topics. True peace is achieved only when relationships reach a level of genuine depth. While we should not necessarily pick fights with people to interact more deeply, neither should we be afraid to engage in dialogue that prompts us to work through more intimate material. Unless they are skilled professionals, people who sing vocal harmonies do not always hit their notes right away. There may be a period during which notes can't be found or clash with other tones. This can be frustrating, but after some effort the differences can be worked out. Once they are, the results can be beautiful to perform and wonderful to hear.

MAINTAINING FOCUS

Focus is an interesting idea. The construct of focus can relate to photography; consider a situation in which an image is blurry and settings must be adjusted to establish clarity. Focus can also relate to how people approach their work. The descriptor of a "focused" individual may refer to someone who is able to stay dedicated and committed, even amidst distraction. Our focus can partially be impacted by our attitude, but we must also establish and maintain structures that keep us on task.

I remain optimistic that we as a church can continue to grow and establish patterns of meaningful, productive conversation. Despite that optimism, there is the realistic understanding that this is going to require a lot of work. There will be many conversations. In addition, there will be some steps forward and some steps back. Truthfully, I get discouraged sometimes because people don't seem to care about making the world a more redeemed place. They are content to enjoy their spoils of life and avoid conflict. They don't want to bother with difficult people.

This is where focus plays a key role. Whether through accountability or encouragement, we can stay on a path. This is also where we again see the vital role of the Holy Spirit. A humanistic approach would suggest that all our drive and dedication must come from within our own source or energy. As followers of Christ, we remember that God is the maker and sustainer of all things. In Philippians 4:13 Paul proclaims that "I can do all things through him who strengthens me." That motivation must be in our heart, always and forever.

MOMENTS OF PAUSE

Sustained effort can take a toll, and sometimes there are situations when continually pushing forward can be counterproductive. Dialogue is something we should constantly pursue, but there may be moments when we should step back, pause the conversation, reassess, and engage in a process of self-reflection. This is again an opportunity for us to evaluate a variety of the factors we have been talking about in earlier chapters. Just because we feel as though we are doing the right thing doesn't mean that we haven't become lost in a stubborn pursuit of our own agenda and fixed mindset.

The challenge is that a short break can turn into a very long gap. In some cases a break can end a promising project. There is value to Sabbath, but we are also prone to procrastination and enjoying a time of rest and relaxation that is free from stress and difficulty. We can easily convince ourselves that we just aren't ready to go back to work, and this may mask a larger problem of lost motivation and drive.

A key aspect of taking breaks is that they allow us to evaluate the factors that have led to this point. Are we taking a break from an individual conversation or larger project because we've encountered pushback? Or an obstacle? These distractions are inevitable, and they are part of a larger process of moving forward and navigating a variety of hurdles. In other words, do we feel the need to take a break simply because we are tired or discouraged? Or is there a strategic reason to step away, which will be followed by a planned and intentional reentry into the process?

BEYOND THE BOOK

I don't know where you will go from here. I'm glad that you are reading the book, but after you finish the last page what will you do? Will you act and pursue a measurable change? If I may issue a challenge, I encourage you to do so. There is no time like the present. Resist the temptation to believe that good intentions are enough and that you will get to things eventually.

There are many ways in which you can get started. Putting anything into action and designing intentional systems of sustained dialogue require not only tasks and timetables but also accountability. There is value in working through a time of planning, such as via workshops, committees, and meetings. Ultimately, you may be the one who acts.

Think about the possibility of creating your own dialogue project, through which you intend to build a relationship that may be difficult to develop over time. To accomplish this, you must maintain patience. Perhaps this may lead to a discussion series, but the key is bringing in people who don't always agree. If the dialogue turns into an extended version of an existing echo chamber, the prospect of true change may be limited.

In Acts 4:34–35 we read of the early church "that there were no needy persons among them. For from time to time those who owned land or houses sold them, brought the money from the sales and put it at the apostles' feet, and it was distributed to anyone who had need." I have always been curious about this passage. Did this happen often? What did it take to get to this point? Was this status difficult to sustain? And were there members of the community who resisted or didn't participate?

If we go back to the passage in Philippians, we can dream of those types of outcomes. The church in Acts has an almost utopian description, though perhaps this wasn't as amazing as it sounds. What we do know is that God is faithful and that, with Him, anything is possible. To get started we must be willing to take the first step and let God lead us.

TEAMWORK AND ACCOUNTABILITY

Acting does not mean that you must do everything on your own. The whole point of bringing people together is to . . . wait for it . . . bring people together! There may be moments when you must take the lead on a conversation or a project, but ultimately it must be a team effort. Involving other people in the process not only increases the wisdom of perspectives but allows the work to be distributed.

I mentioned accountability in the last section. *Accountability* can be an interesting word. Much as with many other constructs, people often talk conveniently about accountability for other people, but they don't necessarily know how to achieve it.

In the workplace the most measurable and extreme form of accountability may be the threat of being fired. We don't necessarily want to have a termination mindset when it comes to fostering dialogue, though there may be times when we must take stock of how serious we are about moving forward.

Much like the construct of accountability partners, the purpose of this mechanism is to provide an impactful process of challenge and support. Accountability partners do not have to be unkind, but whether in a spiritual or vocational realm, an accountability partner is tasked with saying, "Hey, I thought you were going to get this done! What is your progress? Why aren't you working on this? What is holding you up?" In some cases an accountability partner may ask the important question of "How can I help you make this happen?" That can often result in a wonderful balance between accountability and true support.

START WITH ONE

In the movie *Justice League*, a group of united superheroes reach a climactic moment when they must face off against a massive horde of enemies. Batman, a seasoned veteran of many battles, is unfazed. The Flash is relatively new to the superhero business and expresses his anxieties to Batman. The two characters have this brief conversation:

> The Flash: "It's really cool you guys seem ready to do battle and stuff, but, full transparency, I've never done battle. I've just pushed some people and run away."
> Batman: "Save one."
> The Flash: "What?"
> Batman: "Save one person."

The Flash: "Uh. . . which one?"
Batman: "Don't talk, don't fight. Get in, get one out."
The Flash: "And then?"
Batman: "You'll know."

The caveat to this concept is that we can quickly limit ourselves. We can convince ourselves that because we have taken a step forward, we don't have to go much further. One conversation will do, and if we've got that one project, we don't have to think about anything else. Perhaps that is your calling, but we must be careful that we do not limit God's plan for our life.

People often talk about their capacity, but you may have capacity beyond what you think you do, and God will equip you. The Bible is filled with characters who resisted God, questioned their own ability to perform, and in some cases ran away. Despite all the crystal-clear situations in which God was right and humans were wrong, we can keep doubting. God puts up with a lot and doesn't give up on us. We won't match God for tenacity or endurance, and we should always remember that we are sinners, though saved by grace. We do not deserve God's love, so the least we can do is put forth a sustained effort of obedience. We are called to serve our calling and build relationships with other people, while maintaining a sense of gratitude for what we have been given.

A CALL TO FAITHFULNESS

It is often good to be results-oriented. In Western society we tend to evaluate success numerically. Some of that can be a good framework because we are able to objectively know when we have achieved certain results. The difficulty is that we can convince ourselves that we are successful as Christ followers only if we produce certain outcomes. That is not a scriptural perspective. We are called to be faithful and obedient and to keep listening for God's call. We can still go for big outcomes that can be quantified with earthly measurements. We can aim for large-scale impact but know that God does not grade on output. He grades on obedience.

This may be disappointing to some. We want to feel a sense of legacy, a sense that our efforts are going toward a fruitful outcome. I would remind you that our role may be small or large but that God will always use a servant who cheerfully and willingly seeks His will, even if the task is difficult. God is the same yesterday, today, and tomorrow. That is comforting and exciting. Happy dialoguing. When you get stuck, don't think. Just pray.

PRACTICAL TIP

In terms of conversation and projects, write down what you want to accomplish by the end of the week, month, and year. Give your goals to someone and ask them to hold you accountable.

DISCUSSION QUESTIONS

1. What (or who) is the object of your next dialogue project?
2. What will you do to overcome obstacles, resistance, tension, and fatigue?
3. What does it look like for you to be a catalyst in inspiring your community group?
4. What are you going to do today to change the world?

BIBLIOGRAPHY

CHAPTER 1

Arnold, Jack, director. *The Brady Bunch.* Season 4, episode 18, "The Subject Was Noses." Aired February 9, 1973, on ABC.

Boyle, Gregory. *Tattoos on the Heart: The Power of Boundless Compassion.* Riverside: Free Press, 2010.

Kimball, Dan. *They like Jesus but Not the Church: Insights from Emerging Generations.* Grand Rapids: Zondervan, 2007.

Lewis, C. S. *Mere Christianity.* Jerusalem: Dolphin, 1969.

Perkins, John. *One Blood: Parting Words to the Church on Race and Love.* Chicago: Moody Publishers, 2018.

CHAPTER 2

Singer, Bryan, director. *Superman Returns.* Burbank, CA: Warner Bros. Pictures, 2006.

CHAPTER 3

Bruckheimer, Jerry, director. *Pirates of the Caribbean - the Curse of the Black Pearl.* Burbank, CA: Walt Disney Studios, 2003.

Capra, Frank, director. *It's a Wonderful Life.* Los Angeles, CA: RKO Radio Pictures, 1946.

Darabont, Frank, director. *The Shawshank Redemption*. Burbank, CA: Warner Bros. Pictures, 1994.

O'Connor, Gavin, director. *Miracle*. Burbank, CA: Walt Disney Pictures, 2004.

Wilson, Dave, director. *Saturday Night Live*. Season 16, episode 12, "Daily Affirmations with Stuart Smalley." Aired February 9, 1991, on NBC.

CHAPTER 4

Haidt, Jonathan. *The Righteous Mind: Why Good People Are Divided by Politics and Religion*. New York: Vintage Books, 2013.

Liman, Doug, director. *The Bourne Identity*. Universal City, CA: Universal Pictures, 2002.

CHAPTER 5

Lucas, George, director. *Star Wars: Episode II – Attack of the Clones*. Century City, CA: 20th Century Fox, 2002.

Lucas, George, director. *Star Wars: Episode IV – A New Hope*. Century City, CA: 20th Century Fox, 1977.

CHAPTER 6

"Crystal Pepsi." The Soda Wiki. Accessed January 13, 2023. https://thesoda.fandom.com/wiki/Crystal_Pepsi.

CHAPTER 7

Medina, John. *Brain Rules: 12 Principles for Surviving and Thriving at Work, Home, and School*. Seattle: Pear Press, 2008.

The Myers & Briggs Foundation – MBTI® basics. Accessed January 13, 2023. https://www.myersbriggs.org/my-mbti-personality-type/mbti-basics/.

CHAPTER 8

History.com Editors. "Watergate Scandal." History.com. A&E Television Networks, October 29, 2009. https://www.history.com/topics/1970s/watergate.

Hoffer, Eric. *The True Believer: Thoughts on the Nature of Mass Movements*. New York, Perennial Classics, 2002.

CHAPTER 9

Golding, William. *Lord of the Flies*. London: Faber and Faber, 1954.

CHAPTER 10

Chesterton, G. K. *The Father Brown Omnibus*. New York: Dodd, Mead and Company, 1935.

Coen, Joel and Ethan, directors. *The Big Lebowski*. Universal City, CA: Gramercy Pictures, 1998.

Doran, G. T. (1981). "There's a S.M.A.R.T. way to write management's goals and objectives." *Management Review*. 70 (11): 35–36.

Hess, Jared. *Napoleon Dynamite*. Century City, CA: Fox Searchlight Pictures, 2004.

Jacobellis v. Ohio, 378 U.S. 184 (1964).

Lennon, John. "Imagine." Apple, 1971.

Robinson, Phil Alden, director. *Sneakers*. Universal City, CA: Universal Studios, 1992.

CHAPTER 12

"About APU: Our Motto." About APU – Azusa Pacific University. Accessed January 13, 2023. https://www.apu.edu/about/motto/.

"Franklin D. Roosevelt." The White House. The United States Government, December 23, 2022. https://www.whitehouse.gov/about-the-white-house/presidents/franklin-d-roosevelt/.

"Home." I Am Second, January 13, 2023. https://www.iamsecond.com/.

Parker, Oliver, director. *An Ideal Husband*. Santa Monica, CA: Icon Productions, 1999.

Spheeris, Penelope, director. *Wayne's World*. Hollywood, CA: Paramount Pictures, 1992.

The Myers-Briggs Company. Thomas-Kilmann Conflict Mode Instrument (TKI® Assessment). Accessed January 13, 2023. https://www.themyersbriggs.com/en-US/Products-and-Services/TKI.

CHAPTER 13

Elliot, T.S. *Four Quartets*. New York: Harcourt, 1943.

French, J. R. P., Jr., and Raven, B. H. (1959). The bases of social power. In D. Cartwright (Ed.), *Studies in Social Power* (pp. 150–167). Ann Arbor, MI: Institute for Social Research.

Snyder, Zack, director. *Justice League*. Burbank, CA: Warner Bros. Pictures, 2017.

Made in the USA
Monee, IL
24 February 2023